TRANSLAND

TRANSLAND

CONSENT, KINK & PLEASURE

MX. SLY

ARSENAL PULP PRESS
VANCOUVER

ARSENAL PULP PRESS
Suite 202 – 211 East Georgia St.
Vancouver, BC V6A 1Z6
Canada
arsenalpulp.com

The publisher gratefully acknowledges the support of the Canada Council for the Arts
and the British Columbia Arts Council for its publishing program and the Government of
Canada and the Government of British Columbia (through the Book Publishing Tax Credit
Program) for its publishing activities.

Arsenal Pulp Press acknowledges the xʷməθkʷəy̓əm (Musqueam), Sḵwx̱wú7mesh
(Squamish), and səlilwətaɬ (Tsleil-Waututh) Nations, custodians of the traditional, ancestral,
and unceded territories where our office is located. We pay respect to their histories,
traditions, and continuous living cultures and commit to accountability, respectful relations,
and friendship.

The following essays were previously published in a different form:

"Cling Wrap," originally published as "When queer sexual mentorship comes in the form
of cling wrap" in *Xtra Magazine*, December 8, 2016

"Rope Bondage," originally published as "Japanese rope bondage taught me that kink bonds
last forever" in *Xtra Magazine*, April 7, 2017

"Piss Play," originally published as "How piss play helped me get over childhood shame"
in *Xtra Magazine*, April 24, 2017

"F to X, not F to M," originally published as "The question of my trans-ness has a complicated
answer" in *Xtra Magazine*, October 4, 2018

Cover art and text design by Jazmin Welch
Edited by Catharine Chen
Proofread by Alison Strobel

Printed and bound in Canada

Library and Archives Canada Cataloguing in Publication:
Title: Transland : consent, kink & pleasure / Mx. Sly.
Names: Sly, Mx., author.
Identifiers: Canadiana (print) 20230221947 | Canadiana (ebook) 2023022198X |
    ISBN 9781551529318 (softcover) | ISBN 9781551529325 (EPUB)
Subjects: LCSH: Sly, Mx. | LCSH: Bondage (Sexual behavior) | LCSH: Sexual excitement. |
    LCSH: Gender-nonconforming people—Canada—Biography. | LCGFT: Autobiographies.
Classification: LCC HQ79 .S59 2023 | DDC 306.77/5—dc23

For my cheerleader and BFF, *Elma*

Transland is a memoir and a work of creative non-fiction.

The names of some people, events, and places have been changed to protect the identities of those involved.

A list of reader content warnings appears at the end of this book.

CONTENTS

CLING WRAP

"Can we try a mummification scene?"

Sam and I are at a sex-on-premises venue called Fountain, in downtown Toronto. It's women-and-trans-only night. The door to Fountain is tucked away off the main street, and the red light beside the door is the only thing that makes an impression against its grey stucco exterior. Inside it's brightly lit, with pale-yellow walls and scuzzy anti-slip floors near a ground-floor hot tub and scuzzy carpeted stairs leading to more play spaces above. Every room is themed: the room with dungeon equipment is where fetish is more welcome, and the room that's got beaded curtains and half a camper van in it is where aging swingers can reclaim their glory days. Fountain is an inner-city conversion of an older three-storey mini-mansion, with a Juliet balcony overlooking a backyard grotto. At one point, this was a family home. Inside Fountain, the air smells like chlorine, vinyl, surface cleaner, and cunt.

Women-and-trans-only night at Fountain has a different vibe than any other event the sex club runs. There are way more people wearing clothing, for one thing. There's a lot more tentativeness. There's a lot less fucking. There's a surplus of fresh, clean towels available—no cis dudes means there are just a lot fewer people present. There's a sense of cooperation and awkwardness, like a crowd of strangers waiting for the elevator. A lot more icebreakers that never break the ice. There's a Twister mat spread out on the floor next to a stripper pole, and the Twister mat's more in demand than the stripper pole is. There are always a lot more first-timers feeling out the milieu and themselves. Sam is a first-timer. I'm not.

Sam and I met six months ago, in Vancouver, where she lives. She's a twenty-three-year-old actor with blond hair and blue eyes, and her special acting skills include being young, being hot, and playing the ukulele. She's eloquent in the way young women with a lot of privilege are, especially the ones who have just finished theatre school. Real life hasn't set in. She has enough free time at her front-of-house job to read queer feminist literature and to imagine herself as the next queer feminist icon before biking to an audition and then sleeping over at her straight older boyfriend's place. She's aware that she's conventionally pretty and interested in complicating her looks enough that she feels unique and alternative, while also preserving her looks enough that she'll never have to face how this world really treats women it deems ugly. She's haunted by the fear that people don't take her seriously but never interrogates whether or not she should be. The day I meet her, she flips her blond hair, rolls her blue eyes, and complains, "I'm always cast as the beautiful ingenue," without a drop of irony.

In a lot of ways, Sam is the person I dreamt of being when I was a tween, reading *Seventeen* magazine and living in my imagination as much as possible. I envy Sam's ease in life. When I was a kid, I'd drool over the magazine articles and picture a different life for myself instead of dwelling on the fact that I'd go to school thinking I had a tan and realize later that I was just dirty. Nothing in *Seventeen* ever talked about cycles of abuse in families or criminal neglect, and I wanted to live in that world, free from violence and complexity, so badly. I feel drawn to Sam because, while twenty-nine-year-old me can tell that she's a narcissist, thirteen-year-old me still thinks she's a cover model, and I haven't outgrown being driven by the safety I wanted when I was thirteen. I'm also drawn to Sam because she's too self-involved to ever look at me closely. I dissociate from reality fairly often, and while that's not a good thing, it takes less effort to roll with dissociating than it would to improve my mental health. The upside to hanging out with narcissists when you're unwell is that they so rarely push you to be happy.

Months into a casual Facebook friendship with Sam, she messages that she's headed to Toronto for a visit and asks me if I know any BDSM-type parties that will be happening while she's in town.

All of my Facebook friends know I'm bossy bottom who likes sting pain, even if they have no idea what that means. My timeline is a smorgasbord of kinky TMIs. I make my sex life my defining characteristic online because, in my own ways, I also want to prove that I'm unique and alternative. Mostly, I crave an enticing way of telling the world there is something inside me that is not okay. My hope is that if my pain is titillating, maybe it will be worth paying attention to.

Sam texts me that she's slapped someone's face a couple times during sex and thinks that might mean she's a dominatrix. I don't tell her how naive she sounds, or how often women like her expect me to facilitate their journeys of sexual self-discovery. Instead, thirteen-year-old me offers up a list of sex-friendly events and locations.

I'm bi and kinky. When you're bi, kinky, and talk about your sex life publicly, you get about an inch of space to figure yourself out before people start asking you to figure out their sex lives for them too. I want to tell people like Sam that I'm not a tour guide—this is just my life, I don't live to facilitate anyone else's self-discovery—but I'm also afraid that if I don't give people what they want, I'll disappear from their minds completely. It's a tension I navigate without elegance. I let in people who don't deserve it, then hate myself for it later.

With Sam, I assume I'll show her around Fountain, introduce her to some people who are reliable humans, and that'll be it. I've been down this road with queer people like her before, the kind who say "cishet" like it's a pejorative but are very comfortable using people just like the grossest cishet dudes. When Sam talks to me I know I'm a vehicle, not a destination.

Sam and I arrive at Fountain. We put on our club outfits. Sam dresses to impress in black lingerie. I strip down to skin and unkempt pubic hair and stay that way. I give Sam a mini-tour, then she wanders off on her own—and I figure that I'm dismissed for the night now that I've facilitated what Sam wanted access to.

I join a line to try out a Sybian the club has brought in. A Sybian is like a pony-sized saddle you can attach a variety of dildos to. You slide whatever orifices you enjoy onto the dildos until you're sitting astride the saddle. Then, you or someone else picks up the Sybian's remote control and starts playing with the toy's vibrate functions. Sybians offer deep penetration, with prostate and G spot rocking available. People who are into Sybians are *really* into Sybians. At Fountain, whenever a Sybian is brought in, it's set up on a stage so that even if you line up all night but don't get a chance to ride, at least you get a chance to watch.

"Why are you holding a piece of cling wrap across your body?" Sam asks, sliding in next to me.

"If I get a turn on the Sybian, I'm going to use this to make a DIY saddle condom. I'm trying to keep the cling wrap from clinging to itself so I can use it to avoid a yeast infection."

The person in line behind me looks annoyed—I'm not sure if it's because Sam's cut in or because in sex-positive situations, it's bad form to admit that public play can come with a health price tag.

"It's a good look on you."

"I guess I look like the opening moments of a mummification scene."

"What's a mummification scene?"

The first time I saw someone mummified was at a lesbian-run fetish event called Feast Unleashed that happens over Canadian Thanksgiving every year. Fetish events, especially lesbian-run ones, tend to have groanworthy names. I imagine them emerging from some group chat of lesbians who've found each other through friends, metamours, and yarn bombing collectives. Mostly women in academia, with maybe a peppering of work in social justice, and that discussion of "what do we call our fetish event?" happens between sharing pictures of cats and posting links to Fluevog shoes. Lesbian kink events are the height of hummus-fuelled middle-aged dyke nerd culture—and while I poke fun at it, I'm also in love with it.

Feast Unleashed is promoted almost exclusively through word of mouth, and people come to Toronto from across North America to attend. The hotels near its venue book up with queer tops, bottoms, and switches lugging suitcases full of wet wipes, piss pads, needle-play gear, and whips. At check-in at the start of the weekend, hugs are exchanged between folks who haven't seen each other since the last Feast and giggles shared about explaining nipple clamps to the TSA. Feasters treat the airport interrogation like a badge of honour. I can never tell if that's really what it feels like for them, though, or if the giggles are covering up the fact that no matter how hard-core a masochist someone is, it still hurts to have your sex life pawed through by airport security, because it's an abstract pat-down of your soul.

I'd thought I had a broad sense of what people are into sexually, until my first Feast. By day I sat through sex discussions run by human ponies. By night I watched twenty-person circle jerks in dungeons that were just a prelude to an even bigger all-night, all-queer gang bang. I watched buckets of thick, buttery lube disappear into a person's cunt all night long while she happily swung back and forth in a sex swing. I watched a leather daddy lie on the floor and deep throat her wife's eight-inch stiletto heel for an hour while her wife sat on a chair above, fondling her own clit—both of them just loving it. Whether you're down to fuck or just down to lurk and linger, spending a weekend with the ladies of Feast Unleashed changes your reality permanently.

Practised in its most basic form, mummification is a fetish that involves wrapping a person so they are completely immobilized, in anything from fabric to latex to chains. The first time I see someone mummified, it's past 3 a.m. on a Sunday night, and things at Feast Unleashed are winding down. I'm wandering around, taking in the dwindling dungeon play, and I come across a very quiet three-person mummification scene tucked away in a back corner.

One person is lying on a table while two others move around them silently. The person lying on the table is being wrapped in cling wrap from foot to face, so tightly they can barely wiggle a pinky. There's a pinprick hole in the wrap at their mouth so they can breathe through a cocktail straw that's been poked through. Their dominants walk around the table, pinching them, slapping them, four hands moving over their immobilized body. Now a pinch to inside of their arm, now a push into their stomach, now a slap to their face, now a fingernail along their thigh—while the cling wrap holds them down, holds their eyes closed, and holds off any reality other than just feeling.

I stand a few feet away and watch the world get pared to a cocktail straw, breath, and whatever language one thinks in when allowed to experience sensation without the ability or responsibility to respond to it.

I'd never seen or imagined the B in BDSM—bondage—being executed with such stillness. It was one of the many times that, for me, fetish has blurred the boundary between sensuality and sexuality. Afterward I rode the streetcar home, full of wonder. If you can have a mind-shattering experience by means of being immobilized on a table, without anyone ever touching your crotch, is sex, sexual orientation, or gender really that important? If sensual experience can live outside of relationships, gender roles, and other social constructs that come with a bunch of baggage, does that make sensuality more interesting than sex?

I was high on the mummification scene, and all I'd done was watch it. It exposed me to a new way of engaging with my body, and I wanted it.

I tell Sam this story while we're at the front of the line, watching a person scream her head off atop the Sybian.

"Can we try a mummification scene?" Sam asks.

"You want to mummify me?"

As we tumble into negotiating the terms of our scene—Sam topping, me bottoming—something's different than it's been in our past conversations. She knows I'm a sub because I am— but in the past, when she's claimed to be a dom, I've heard her confusing a point of view with an aesthetic. My impression has always been that Sam sees dominance as a costume and an acting role, as opposed to how I understand it. Whether someone's a top, bottom, dominant, submissive, switch, big, or little, for me BDSM isn't about turning a look or fitting into a role—it's a way of acknowledging the discordant absurdity of reality and trying to deal with it.

When I've called a person my dominant, it has less to do with what they wear or the codes of how we interact and more to do with the fact that their presence makes me feel safe because they make me feel less alone. Sure, there's a set of styles kinksters tend to adopt, like the lacy French maid, the biker chick, the steampunk goth, the pvc-clad *Matrix* wannabe—which is the category I sometimes fall into—but the look isn't the point. The look is hanky code. The look is peacocking. The look is just a way of communicating what's on the inside, which is partly about proclivities—are you a sub or a dom, are you into medical play, do you want to be degraded—but underneath that, what's really on the inside is a sense that there's something missing day to day. What's on the inside is the sense that getting together with friends, getting a degree, paying bills, receiving Amazon deliveries, achieving upward social mobility—vanilla life—is just an act of pretending.

The thigh-high boots, the assless chaps, and the leather collars can be the way we say to each other, "I'm tired of pretending too." The aesthetics of kink are a wordless plea: can we please be strange and weird enough together that it cuts through the banal bullshit we all pretend to be invested in, and for a moment, can we be something real?

When I lock eyes with someone in a dungeon and immediately feel like I know them, what I see in them is a shared existential yearning, even though I rarely learn their postal code or their real name.

I'm not quite there with Sam; we aren't having a Neo and Trinity moment. But as we talk about what a mummification scene is and how we could play it out, it's the first time Sam stops talking at me and starts speaking with me. We slip from her being the popular girl and me being the band geek into being equals, and for the first time, she lets me show her what I know about fetish, consent, and mutual responsibility as play partners without making me wade through her self-aggrandizing.

We talk about the parameters of what we are open to. I play with strangers often enough that I have my boundaries memorized like a stump speech, so I dig in.

"I don't play with humiliation. I don't like to be laughed at or made fun of, ever. I don't want to hear what you think about the way I look, even if you think you're paying me a compliment. During the scene, no one else talks to me, comes near me, or touches me—and if someone tries to, you have to stop them. I like sting pain, not thud pain. Thud pain is like being hit with a baseball bat. Thud pain makes me angry, and it takes me out of the moment. If I feel thud pain, the scene will end immediately. I like sting pain, pain that lives on the surface. Light spanks over and over on the same place. Pain that makes your skin pink but doesn't leave black bruising. Pain that's about irritating nerve endings. I don't play with consensual non-consent. I don't use safe words because I don't ever play with the idea that I'm giving up my autonomy. When I say no, it always means no. When I say stop, it always means stop. The words I say always have meaning. After the scene, I like aftercare. Usually that means holding me while I come down, making sure I have what I need, and making sure I don't have to interact with anyone other than you until I've exited subspace."

I love the rules-of-play stump speech I give to the randoms I hook up with at fetish events—and now to Sam. It's a list of how I want to play, but it's also a list of how I'd like to be treated every moment of my life. Kink normalizes the idea that people will be happy to hear your boundaries, and I love that about kink, because deep down I wish I could have a rules-of-play conversation with my entire existence.

"What's subspace?" Sam asks. It's the first time someone has asked me this question.

Subspace is difficult to define. Some folks compare subspace to an orgasm in that what it feels like for everyone is unique, but subspace is so much bigger and better than coming. What can distinguish a BDSM scene from a genuinely harmful act is that all the pain a sub experiences in a scene, whether light or intense, short lived or longer lasting, is driving toward inducing subspace.

Some people describe subspace as euphoria. When I'm in subspace, I don't feel like I have an age, a career, or a bank account balance. I don't feel like I have responsibilities, fears, or aspirations. I don't have a past or a future or any dread. Sometimes I don't even feel like I have a body. When I'm in subspace, I just feel like I'm pure energy, a state of nothingness and everythingness all at once.

It feels fucking amazing.

In subspace, I'm free of personhood—and the only thing that binds me to the knowledge I may still be a person is the complete devotion I feel to the person facilitating this feeling.

Physically, the pain, sensation, or social dynamic that's occurring in the scene is activating the sub's sympathetic nervous system, which is responsible for the body's fight-or-flight response, flooding the sub with a release of adrenalin, endorphins, and dopamine. As a result, even if I can still register pain while in subspace, I feel very far away from it. I don't have any problems. Everything feels like it's just going to be all right for the rest of existence, and I don't need to do anything or be anything in particular to assure that outcome. Everything just always has been and always will be okay.

It's a feeling that means the world to me because it's not a feeling I've ever had as a kid. As long as I can remember, I've always been worried.

What subspace means to me is too important for me to trust Sam with it. The experiences that matter most are weighty, like objects, and if I hand them to someone who won't understand, it's like watching them get crumpled in a fist and thrown away.

"I can't explain subspace, Sam."

"Okay. I'll still play the way you want to."

We drop the deep stuff and get down to how we're going to make this scene work.

"Will the bar staff give us a whole roll of cling wrap?"

"Maybe the Dollarama down the street is still open."

"Do you think they'd put cling wrap on my bar tab?"

"I'm googling some nearby grocery store hours."

Our dynamic shifts. Sam and I are like high school besties now; armed with our inside jokes, it's us against the world. Like teens, we're unrelenting in our ego fulfillment. We look around the third floor—there's a bar there that isn't staffed. We hoist ourselves over the bar counter, find a whole unopened box of cling wrap in one cupboard, a pair of scissors in another, and then we crawl back over the bar counter, giggling, while nearby a couple presses pause on having sex to look at us like we're delinquents.

One half of the mid-coitus couple asks us, "You're stealing from the bar and you *aren't* stealing booze?"

I answer, super petulantly, "Have some imagination!"

We head down to the second floor again. The Sybian show is still in full swing. We peek in: someone has just ejaculated, and there's a community effort in process to mop up the jizz.

I tell Sam we should do our scene in the dungeon equipment room. Even though Fountain is fetish friendly, the friendliness of individuals at the club is a spectrum, and if we play in the dungeon, we're less likely to deal with gawkers or complaints. You'd think folks who fuck in public wouldn't pearl-clutch over kink, but bizarrely, there are plenty of people who see liberation as a narrow stream instead of an ocean.

The dynamic between Sam and me shifts again. Even though I'm about to play the role of the submissive in our scene, I'm also the mentor. I'm the one who knows where we should play and the unwritten rules of the space, and I'm the one who can show Sam what to do.

In vanilla life, this scenario plays out constantly in movies: the older woman shows the young sexually inexperienced guy how to fuck. Unlike the cishet trope, sexual mentorship holds a deeper significance for queers than just learning what sex is.

While there are plenty of places where no parent can pretend that being bi or gay will ruin their kid's life, being queer is still looked on as other than predominant. People are still presumed straight until otherwise proven. Hopefully the Gen Alphas and Betas will see all us Millennials retiring to lives filled with basic income rights and legally recognized polycules, but until we get there, coming out is still necessary. Which means that queer sex is still a pushback against the norm, and when mutual desire means that one queer wants to show another what queer sex is for the first time, it's a come-to-Jesus moment: being queer won't always be easy, but it does give us an advantage.

When someone shows us how to have queer sex, we're indebted in a way the young cishet guy in the movie never is, because the sex isn't the point. The sex is an organic and secondary aspect of showing a person how exciting it is to step outside of predominant paradigms of pleasure. Once we step outside of that paradigm, queer sex offers the realization that in the most intimate ways, we are only limited in life by what we can imagine. Queer sexual mentorship offers up the revelation that being queer isn't about being disenfranchised—it's about creative self-authorship. The same is true about sexual mentorship in queer kink.

When I was fresh meat in the queer fetish scene, it was the middle-aged leather dykes I met at Fountain who taught me that red, yellow, and green—traffic signals—are universal check-in terms in a dungeon. It was leather dykes who remarked on how little I seemed to know about everything BDSM, who told me to attend Feast Unleashed, who suggested I create a FetLife account—and who then had to explain that FetLife is like Facebook without any of the rules about nipples and nudity. It was leather dykes who taught me and are still teaching me that it's not true I can't come hard—I just need the right sensory input and psychological circumstance to come hard. It was leather dykes who taught me that I have the voracious right to imagine, seek out, and create a context that makes me come my face off, no matter how unrelatable what brings me pleasure is to anyone else. It was leather dykes who showed me that subspace is even sweeter than coming.

It was leather dykes who taught me how to approach kink: play with other adults, ensure informed consent is present, play without coercion or pressure, and play only with reasonable risk. Always be grateful when someone says no, because their no is a gift that keeps everyone safe. These are the only rules. Everything else is creative self-authorship, fair game, and without shame.

There's an unclaimed corner in the dungeon at Fountain, next to an old fireplace. Sam and I step into the five square feet of play space we're claiming and begin to make it our world.

I stand in the centre of our play space. Sam puts the scissors on the mantel and the box of cling wrap on the floor. She realizes she needs the scissors to cut the cling wrap and picks them up off the mantel. She tries to neatly cut the cling wrap like she's doing kitchen prep, then realizes that's not sexy. She stands there, unsure for a moment, then puts the scissors back on the mantel and rips off a piece of the cling wrap with her teeth. It's humanizing to see

Sam flail a bit in the process of figuring out what to do. I watch her with a smile on my face. Cocks are sexy, cockiness isn't. I'll take honest feral fumbling over bravado any day.

"Can I start?" Sam asks.

"Yes."

She looks me in the eyes for a second, then turns her eyes down to my body, and it feels like a cold wave of ocean water on a hot summer day—shocking, for a moment, in its suddenness, but then you feel alive.

"You have great tits," she offers, as she stares at my chest.

I don't remind Sam that I asked her not to make comments about my body. As much as I give my rules-of-play stump speech, I know that when I play with someone for the first time, my boundaries are going to bristle up against their conditioning. Some people are so conditioned to confuse objectifying someone with making things sexy that they can't stop it tumbling out of their mouths. I prefer to play with people who are more self-aware than Sam is—but if I always waited for self-aware play partners, I'd barely play at all.

I lift my arms up over my head like a dancer. Sam places the first a piece of cling wrap across my chest and holds it in place with her forearm while, with her other arm, she reaches around my torso to pull the wrap taut around me. I look at her eyelashes, the ridge of her nostrils, her lips. This is the closest we've ever been to each other. The cling wrap feels flimsy hanging against my skin, like it's barely there at all. She pulls the cling wrap and wraps it around itself for the first time. Now the wrap's not so flimsy. She wraps it around my body a second time, now a third, now a fourth, faster, with more and more ease. Now the cling wrap's not flimsy at all. I love that moment in play when you feel something soft turn hard.

"Sam, there's a bundle of nerves that runs through the armpit. Keep checking in with me about my ability to move my arms. Keep checking in with me about numbness."

"How do I do that?"

"Ask me to move my arms. Touch my arms and ask me if I can feel it. Have me touch my fingers to my thumb, one by one. Ask me if I feel pins and needles anywhere."

"Pins and needles are bad?"

"Pins and needles are always bad in bondage."

"Move your arms."

I dance my fingers up and down the lengths of my arms, above my head.

"Touch each of your fingers to your thumb."

I do, one by one, while looking at her, like a proud little showing off their dexterity.

"Can you feel everything? Any numbness?"

"No numbness. All feeling."

"Can I keep going?"

"Yes."

I'm topping from the bottom; I'm the one who's having things done to them, but I'm also the one running the scene. It might not sound wild, rough, or like the bondage bukkake vids on PornHub, but mummification, like all bondage, is never without risk—of a pinched nerve, of nerve damage, of cut-off circulation. It takes experience as a sub to have the presence of mind to be able to run the scene while very intense sensations are happening in your body. Sam's a first-timer to bondage like this. I'm not.

She rips another piece of cling wrap off the roll.

"Can I wrap your hips?"

I move my feet next to each other, with my ankles out of alignment so that they won't clang together. All scenes are a collaboration, and an experienced bottom makes a scene work as much as an experienced top does.

"Yes. Just make sure I don't fall over."

Sam holds cling wrap against my hip, pulls it across the front of my genitals, and pulls it tight across my ass cheeks.

All of the smugness I'm used to seeing in Sam's face is gone, and it feels like her mind is quiet, focused, and clear. She looks like all she's thinking about is my body and what she's going to do with it. Above my head, I dance my fingers up and down the lengths of my arms again, like I'm at a club and Rihanna's playing.

"All good, no numbness?"

"No numbness. All feeling," I answer.

Sam rips more cling wrap off the roll. I look down at my body. My chest is wrapped tightly, and my hips are wrapped even tighter, with an unwrapped bit in the middle, like I'm a grotesque sausage half-stuffed into its casing. This isn't the pages of *Penthouse*, *Playboy*, or any magazine I've seen. I love looking at my body distorted like this, reconstructed in fragments. I don't feel self-conscious. Sam wants me ugly like this, and it's liberating.

Sam gets more intuitive and confident in her movements. She stands right up against me to stop me from stumbling, bends over to begin wrapping my legs, and then wraps her own legs around mine for leverage to pull the cling wrap tighter. It's so fucking hot when you feel a person use their whole body to do something to yours, like their every muscle, every limb, every movement is, for a moment, dedicated to you.

She wraps me more freely, criss-crossing up my legs to my upper body until my entire torso, from the nipples down, is encased. I can see my cocooned chest sweating and I can feel sweat dripping down between my ass cheeks. Only my feet, arms, head, and shoulders are free. Every other part of me is a stinky little hotdog, steaming in its own juices.

"What do I do now?" Sam asks.

A crowd has formed at the door of dungeon room, watching from behind an invisible velvet rope they've manifested with their collective trepidation. The Sybian's still going, but Sam and I have become the show now.

"We've got an audience."

"You've been pretty loud." Sam grins.

"If you want to, you can slap me."

She slaps the back of my thigh through the cling wrap.

"You can scratch at me through the cling wrap, if you want to."

Her nails claw into the cling, and I feel like I'm unbreakable. She digs her nails into my stomach as hard as she can and, because of the cling, she only just breaks my skin.

"Can I bite you?"

"Yes."

She bites my chest through the plastic, and I'm high on it—high on the endorphins, high on the shock of her teeth biting hard, high on being invincible, high on the heat of the plastic, high on sweating buckets, high on my own self-drenching genitals, and high on the look on Sam's face as she bites me again.

She wants me and she can't get at me. I love that tension. Every day in the world, I give too much of myself to people so they'll want me, and here I am, wanted for being unconsumable, inaccessible, and indestructible. I start laughing, and I can't stop. The audience in the doorway looks like they have no idea what they're watching. I have no intention of explaining. I picture every person watching us heading home afterward on their own streetcar rides, minds racing with wonder.

The details of our scene are endless. The sting pain goes on and on, intensifying as Sam wraps her body around mine so that her clawing, gnawing, and spanking is simultaneous, spread out, unpredictable, and wild, all over me. I am in subspace.

She keeps attacking me until my genitals are swollen, red hot, soaking wet, and my eyes are bleary. I can barely see. I can't believe I was ever annoyed by Sam. What the hell nonsense was I on? Sam is a God, and cling wrap is a goddamn revelation. Her teeth write into my body that I am not my insecurities. My screams announce that she's anything but a delicate ingenue. We are what we decide to be: creative self-authorship.

Sam tears me out of the plastic slowly, with the scissors, her fingernails, and her teeth. She takes her time turning hard bondage into delicate wisps of plastic at my feet. I watch her electric-blue eyes as she braces her body against mine to make sure I don't wobble. She releases my legs from the bondage, and they immediately turn to goo.

What I adore about Sam in this moment has nothing to do with any of the brags she's tried to impress me with and everything to do with her power. Her age, looks, and acting career make her a stereotype of a stereotype so often, but right now, I see anything but a magazine cover. As she breathes hard and my vision becomes less blurry, I look at the sweat in her hairline. I smell her as her limbs keep wrapping around me, tearing into me and catching me at the same time. There's such a wildness in her eyes. She is so much more than what she shrinks herself down to, day to day, to make herself make sense to casting directors. She is so much more than I could ever see. We've cut through the banal bullshit, and it's me who has stopped swapping status markers, stopped judging her, stopped keeping my distance. In this moment, I worship Sam, and in letting go of all of my fear and envy of her, I let go of the sadness and anger I carry in myself.

Bondage can break down status, reinvent it, and allow us to reinvent ourselves. I feel our bodies moving against each other, think for a moment that I feel Sam's rib cage breathing hard, then realize her body is standing still against mine and the ragged breath I'm feeling is my own.

She slowly lowers me to the floor. A purple-haired queer who's been watching our scene edges toward Sam and offers her two water bottles. Women-and-trans-only night at Fountain is like this. Sometimes it's more of a board games night than a strip show, sometimes it's too friendly and awkward to be a turn on, but the flip side is that people are thoughtful and intuitive enough to bring water when one needs it without expecting a conversation or wanting anything in return.

"Sam, ask me to touch all my fingers to my thumbs."

I'm slipping out of subspace and back into the real world, where I keep showing Sam what to do so that if she's ever playing with a less-experienced sub than me, she'll know what to do, and they'll both have a safer time because of it.

"Touch all your fingers to your thumbs. All good?"

"All good. Greener than good. Greenest green."

We sit for a bit. Sam cleans up the bits of cling wrap. I sip water and stare at the floor in front of me, aware that there are other scenes going on, but at the same time, I'm a world away. I'm grateful for our play and grateful for this shift in how we treat and understand each other. We head down to the showers. Sam gets naked, and I eat her out in the shower while she shampoos her hair.

Suddenly, she goes back to the way she usually is: self-obsessed and self-interested. She doesn't ask me how the claw marks she's left across my chest feel or want to talk about the scene. I ask her if she has a safe plan for getting back to her Airbnb. She doesn't ask me how I'm getting home safely, even though by this point I'm exhausted. Instead she tells me I was great at going down on her and then starts talking about all the cool things she's going to do with other people the next day. It's a shock to my system, like a cold ocean wave that's suddenly bigger than you expected it to be. All the status markers that separate us come pouring back in. Most people prefer not to feel dismissed after sex, but it's particularly hard to weather that dismissal when physical injuries, even consensual ones, begin to ache. My body hurts postplay, and I know how to weather that. I'm disappointed to be weathering my heart hurting too.

For some of us, a BDSM scene is a profound, paradigm-shifting experience and a meaningful part of our intimate relationships. For others, it's just a sexy, risqué thing to do. BDSM can bring up such intense emotions that sometimes it's difficult to understand a scene won't necessarily change the nature of a relationship or form a deeper understanding where before there was only a shallow one. It's hard to wrestle with wondering if what I felt was real, if now that the scene's over, it's changed nothing. It's part of the cheat of playing out a BDSM scene and of tapping into the sympathetic nervous system, because the chemical reality of it in the body is very real, but the social circumstances of it can be an act of pretending. But while a scene can't necessarily change a relationship with another person, it can change the relationship you have with yourself, if you want it to.

I begin to think about my own tendency of people-pleasing and whether quick access to endorphins in a scene is always worth it. I begin to think about how good subspace feels, and how rough it is weathering the drop from it alone. I log on to FetLife and scroll through other bottoms posting photos of their postplay bruising, like postcards from a destination they were brave enough to go to. It reminds me of standing at the check-in desk at Feast Unleashed, listening to folks laugh a bit too loudly about having to explain their sex lives to the TSA. I edge a bit closer to admitting to myself that I want more than make-the-best-of-it scenes with randoms I pick up play with at Fountain.

I begin to wring myself out like a dirty dishrag for other people's entertainment a little less.

A while after our night at Fountain, I let Sam know that I don't want to stay in touch with her. Whether because of her or in spite of her, our mummification scene begins to change things. Whatever I feel about Sam, for a night, this young kink newb dommed the fuck out of me. From that night onward, I start wanting something more.

ROPE BONDAGE

Even when Evie tells me I have great breasts, I don't clock that we're on a date.

It's a rainy spring night in Toronto, and Evie and I are at a dumpling house in Chinatown. I've had a crush on her for years, but it's been a long time since I went out with a beautiful woman and a longer time since a beautiful woman noticed me. I've been dressing like a boy lately, which makes me feel more like myself but also makes me feel like I'm either invisible or completely unappealing. I don't get picked up on dance floors anymore the way I did when Lycra body-con was my second skin.

I was raised on Britney Spears music videos, and the lesson I took away from those was that because I was born with a vagina, to be sexy, I had to play up the curves of my body and all the things I could do with them. In my high school life in Toronto, I was the queen of push-up bras and G-strings pulled up over the waist-line of my low-rise skinny jeans. I felt powerful acting out, like a bratty jailbait terror, even though any time I was one-on-one with someone in a sexual situation, I froze, and my cover as a horny, slutty badass was blown. I'd pass around notes to my best friends in English class about the size of our English teacher's dick. I'd unbutton every button of my school polo and feel accomplished when boys asked what it would be like to titfuck me. Dressing provocatively femme felt like it gave me strength, and that strength felt like an innate necessity. Even as a teen, it felt like the only power I'd ever have would come from someone else desiring me— so I wanted to be wanted very badly.

The way the world has changed how it treats me ever since I stopped sexing myself up for attention and the way I don't see myself as a woman anymore is what's on my mind when Evie brings up my breasts. It's been so long since I wore a bra that I mostly forget I have breasts at all, so I don't clock that she's flirting with me. Instead, I clock the differences between us.

Evie describes herself as tomboy femme—it's an accurate description. She always looks like she belongs in a field somewhere, her high ponytail bobbing up and down as she runs away from you. The wind picks up the wispy bits of hair around her face and holds them up around her head like rays of sunlight, or like whiskers. As she looks back at you over her shoulder, you'll notice that one of her eyes is green and the other blue-grey, just before her face splits in a knowing grin and she turns away from you to run off into tall grasses again. Whenever Evie's name comes up, this is my image of her.

She has strong WASPY features and is charming, haughty, and androgynous, like Hugh Grant at twenty, even though Evie's in her late thirties. Her face has an easy stillness that means she rarely accidentally reveals what she's thinking. She has long wheat-coloured hair that's never styled. The once a year she wears makeup, it's a smear of clumpy reddish purple on her lips that makes her look like a young woman playing with makeup for the first time and coming out very pleased with herself. She carries herself with an ageless confidence and ineffable dignity.

She's fit and surprisingly strong, but in a way that's beyond team sports, beyond keeping up with trends, and beyond keeping up with the Kardashians. One day for work she'll be in a hotel room in Japan, and the next she'll be inside a Frank Lloyd Wright–designed private estate in the American Midwest. When she's at home, she lives in the west end of Toronto, in one of the industrial pockets between downtown condos and areas known for being great school districts. Whenever she's out in the world, queers are drawn to her orbit, and cishet men sink to their knees to talk to her and, if they can afford an engagement ring, to attempt to lock that shit down.

Evie is a professional dominatrix. That profession is the sole source of income that funds her existence. Her life revolves around being creatively and violently graceful, and her intimate intuition is honed as if her life depends on it, because it has.

She sees people for who they are on a very deep level, beyond all the facades they put up, and she knows that she can financially thrive in the space between the dirty desires people feel they can't show the world and the scaffolding of who they pretend to be. She has this fascinating way of picking up on the fantasies people ball up within themselves because they're afraid to be judged, and whether she's playing for pay or playing for fun, she knows how to prod, spank, and tease those scenarios to the surface.

I first see Evie across a dungeon at Feast Unleashed, on a Saturday night. She's in the middle of a scene, with her submissive leaning over a spanking bench, face down. Evie moves like she's the star of her own music video, wearing black-leather booty shorts and a black-leather bra. She's spanking her sub's ass with her bare hands while twirling around and flipping her hair like she knows she's going to break the internet with her choreography. Mid-spank-dance move, she spins, turns away from her sub, locks eyes with me, then rubs her black-leather ass against the bright-red ass of her sub while her sub screams. Every muscle around my spine contracts as I look into Evie's eyes and vicariously experience the scrape and thrill of black-leather butt on bare, brutalized ass cheeks.

As Evie twirls away from our eye contact and keeps whaling on her sub's ass, I think about how unscripted her impulses seem—they feel authentic and inherent to her being rather than learned. I can't stop watching and wondering where she gets her gorgeous ideas from and what music videos she grew up watching.

The next day, Evie shows up to Feast Unleashed in a tan-latex minidress with exaggerated shoulders and a huge latex bow on the front. It's so campy that I pounce on it as a conversation starter. She is polite, but our conversation is brief. Later on, she loops back to me and tells me that she's a pro dom—which feels like an intense share—and I gratefully hold on to any intimacy she wants to offer me, even if it's only information. We exchange FetLife handles before she goes off to play out another scene. As I get to know more about her through running into her at dungeon parties, watching her play, and scrolling through what she shares on FetLife, my crush on her deepens because of her grace, her ridiculous outfits, her complete lack of self-consciousness, and because I gradually learn that, like me, she is into rope bondage.

In the public shibari scene—a.k.a. the Japanese rope bondage scene—there are a lot of very specific terms beyond just the Japanese names for certain ties or positions. The person doing the tying is generally referred to the as the "rigger" or the "rope top." The person being tied is referred to as the "rope bottom," "the model," or, more misogynistically, as the "rope bunny," the "doll," or the "rope slut." I've been a rope bottom for three years.

Most shibari scene terms assume the person doing the tying will be a cis guy and the person being tied will be a cis woman—typically petite and thin so her light weight makes him look that much bigger, stronger, and manlier. A lot of the cis guy riggers I've met are insecure about their masculinity. When most of them talk to me, what they see is five feet and a hundred pounds of tieable male ego boost, with their unspoken plan being that I'll give them a blow job somewhere along the way.

A lot of the rope scene reinforces gender binaries and gendered roles rather than subverting the status quo. A lot of the cis dudes in the scene claim to be heteroflexible—not because they'd ever get fucked by another guy, but because they believe it creates the impression that they're less basic than they are and more trustworthy than they are. The greatest form of heteroflexibility present is that most of the straight dudes in the rope scene are deeply emotionally invested in how they're perceived by each other. These riggers leverage their rope skills to fuck hot chicks otherwise outside of their league and try to one-up each other with who they're fucking—as if treating assigned-female-at-birth bodies as status symbols is a novel idea. It's a lot of competition, posturing, and high school politics. I'd stay away from the public shibari scene if it weren't for the fact that, for a rope bottom like me, rope is a drug I can't get enough of.

Most people who are seriously into rope bondage tie with jute rope, which is manufactured from the jute plant. Jute is a long, soft, shiny stalk that grows tall, reaching straight up toward the sun in fields soaked by monsoons. Jute thrives in wet earth and humid heat. Even the plant is sexy.

When I'm being tied, the tension against my skin of individual strands of raw jute wound into rope scratches at all my nerve endings simultaneously, with every movement I make. Rope makes tiny movements feel huge, changing the scale of what it

35

means to attempt something or to feel accomplishment. In rope, even barely perceivable movements release more endorphins than rock climbing for hours would. Tied in rope, every movement in one part of my body is felt somewhere else. Moving an ankle pulls at a bond at my hip. A change of position in my hips tighten bonds at my wrists. There's scratching, bruising, and pressure everywhere. Rope creates little microtears in my skin, mercilessly, everywhere the rope is. When tied, I am very aware of how connected everything is—in the body, between the body and the mind, between the mind and the eternal, and between the eternal and ecstasy.

Tied in jute, I begin to get drunk on the smell of it, so close and enveloping me. The environment it came from will always be trapped in its fibres—it smells earthy and wet. As a rigger pulls rope against itself and around me, jute fibers shed tiny little fragments, covering me in a fine layer of rope dust, and it feels like the universe reminding me where I came from.

For me, rope is like a form of regression therapy, expect I'm not regressing into my childhood. In rope I regress back through the timeline of evolution into primordial ooze, and from there I have the opportunity to snap forward in evolution into a different kind of being entirely. In rope I've transformed into a rabid dog, devolved into having no sex organs at all, and re-evolved into having genders not yet articulated.

In rope I've been wild without worry because, being bound, I can be as wild I want to without the burden of worrying that I'm going to hurt anybody, that I'm going to break anything, or that there are consequences. I've been alive like I was a thought on the tip of someone's tongue, alive like I'm an idea rather than a reality, alive like I could be anything now and snap out of existence in the next moment, so as long as I do exist, I'd better be very fucking loud.

Rope has no sympathy. Once you're inside its bonds, it doesn't loosen up just because the sensation of it on skin is getting overwhelming. Rope is indifferent to you and to your sense of overwhelm, instead beckoning you to become rawer, wilder, and weirder so that you become a new kind of creature capable of sustaining its torture.

The indifference of the rope is healing for me. When I was a kid, my parents' indifference almost killed me and two of my siblings. As kids, our survival was our own responsibility, but being kids, we lacked the agency to make our lives safer. Rope bondage allows me to re-experience evolving to endure and thrive in the face of being trapped in a circumstance indifferent to me. It's empowering because it reminds me where I've been, what I've survived, and that I'll survive whatever life throws at me next.

All of this is what it's like to be high on rope: personal histories and the history of life on this planet all seem to line up on the same page, and singular events bend the page to become the angled creases that transform space and time into a paper crane. I've never been more at peace and more intensely unrestrained in feeling and thought than when I've been intensely restrained. Rope reframes everything.

If rope is a drug, then riggers are my drug dealers.

A year into being a rope bottom, I've only been tied by queer trans and cis women, which means my rope sessions are few and far in between. There aren't many queer riggers in the publicly engaged rope scene, and the tops I tie with live in Montreal, Ottawa, and New York City, just far away enough from my basement apartment in Toronto to be out of regular reach.

I've been fucking straight men for as long as I've been having sex, either perfunctorily for the sake of it or passionately as an act of love, but the thought of being tied up by one of these cisgender rigger guys—and getting pulled into their high school rope world—is nauseating. But a year into being tied, I'm jonesing hard for more bondage. I toss out online that I'm looking to get tied more regularly, and a queer woman I know from Fountain suggests I reach out to a straight-but-cool guy she knows in the scene who goes by the handle Sakura on FetLife. I DM, and he writes back cordially—no creepy vibe, no cis male condescension—and offers to meet up for a chat and a drink.

A quick Google search reveals that Sakura is not casual about rope. He teaches bondage for a living. Looking at photos online, I realize I've seen him tie before onstage at a rope exhibition called the Black Mask Bondage Extravaganza. BMBE is run by a middle-aged guy who styles himself after the sadistic Batman villain Black Mask and who, in spite of this, takes himself very seriously. While Sakura takes rope seriously, he carries himself with his tongue firmly planted in cheek. When I watched Sakura tie at BMBE, he was pissing off every wannabe macho dude present by wearing a Japanese schoolgirl blazer and skirt onstage, like the Street Fighter character of the same name. The other guys there were pissed off not just because he was refusing to engage in compulsory rope top masculinity, but because, even in a skirt and blouse, he was still coming across as the most desirable piece of dick in the place.

When I message Sakura, I've been picking up play mostly with queers who are into rope on the side of their day lives as feminist bookstore owners, airplane mechanics, and waiters. Rope is Sakura's life, full stop. In the realm of rope, he is something completely apart from what I've known, and looking him up before meeting him makes me nervous—not like I'm going on a blind date or a job interview, but like I'm about to meet someone much, much cooler than me, and I don't know what that will mean.

Even though we've looked at pictures of each other online, we exchange ways of recognizing each other. Sakura says he'll be the Aussie with long black hair braided down his back and chipped black nail polish. I say I'll be the bleached blond Canadian pixie boy in Chucks the colour of the red Australian desert.

My earlobes are prickly and my armpits are hot as I wait for him in a tattered booth at Java Joint, a twenty-four-hour diner dive known for cheap prices, serving alcohol to minors, and frequent food poisonings. Sakura slides into the booth seat across from me and holds out his big hand. His palms are so rope-callused I can feel scenes just from touching his fingers.

"Hi, I'm James. How ya doing, sweetie?"

In person and out of his stage persona, James is tall, slender, and strong, with a charisma that wouldn't translate on Instagram but is captivating as fuck, just the same. He's in his thirties, about ten years older than me. He comes across like a former bush kid: wide-eyed, extroverted, always running around, restless and hungry for a world beyond the outback. He dresses like a concert roadie who only wears T-shirts given to him at gigs because that's all he owns. He moves with the confidence of a lion, and when he looks at me, I feel safe and scared at the same time, like a lion cub learning what it means to be.

We make polite chit-chat. I offer to buy him a drink. He offers that he's a recovering addict and orders an herbal tea. We talk about *1984* because I'm in the habit of carrying a novel with me everywhere, and I have it on me. We talk about politics, the capacity people have for Orwellian doublethink, and I share about day-to-day ironies that I clock but most people seem to adamantly ignore.

"Sweetie, the other day I walked by a costume jewellery store called Jealously, and I was the only one who thought it was funny." James grins.

He asks me how flexible I am, what my fitness regime looks like, how long I've been a rope bottom, and who I've been tied by. I answer the way I do whenever I'm in a situation where someone else holds the keys to something I want: truthfully, muddled with what I think the person wants to hear, and offered with self-deprecation that makes it all go down easy.

"Why rope?" James asks.

It's not a question any other rope top has ever asked me.

"In rope, I feel like I understand almost everything—about the universe, about my experiences, about the world around me. The parts left that I don't understand feel small in comparison, like a size I can hold in my hand, and if the things I don't understand are so small that I can hold them, then they're too small to hurt me. That's what rope does for me."

James is quiet for a bit. He pulls a pack of cigarettes out of his pocket and fingers a cigarette as though it were twine while he decides where to take things.

"Your mind really goes flying in rope, sweetie."

I nod. My ass sweats into the tattered diner seat.

"I think we should try a scene."

"Yes!" I say, way too eagerly.

"Floor work only, no suspensions. Nothing too risky. Let's just grapple and see how we like each other."

"Yes! Yeah. Totally."

"Come outside with me."

We stand on a street corner on Queen West at dusk, and a streetcar dings on its way past. James lights up his cigarette and tells me the next time he's free. I pretend to check my schedule—there's no chance I'm not going to meet James whenever he'll have me. He points a block down the street to a bar called the Hideaway, known mostly as a place to score cocaine. He ties in a studio above the Hideaway, he tells me, and we agree to meet outside the bar in a week. We're not colleagues, so we don't shake hands. We're not friends, so we don't hug. I say goodbye, jump on a streetcar, and watch his tall frame get smaller as the streetcar rattles away.

A week later, I sit perched on a newspaper box outside of the Hideaway, waiting for James, creaming my boxers, and trying to mentally prepare for the possibility of whatever is coming, whether it be tying, having another chat, realizing he's a creep, or getting ghosted. James texts that he's on his way back from an NA meeting at a church up the street. It's not a good idea for a recovering addict to work above a drug den, but James is the kind of person who can't stop himself from edging close to the fire even if he doesn't want to get burned. I don't judge him. I'm that kind of person too.

When he sees me, his face splits into a smile that sends ripples through his thick-skinned lion face. He scoops me up off the newspaper box like I weigh nothing, and I hold on to his broad arms in complete comfort. It feels like we've known each other before in another lifetime, in Narnia or in some kind of Terminator-esque the-future-is-the-past situation. He carries me, propped against his chest, up the stairs and through a winding maze of hallways above the Hideaway. Everything with James feels familiar even though he's a stranger.

"Welcome to the Shibari Salon, sweetie."

The door to James's rope studio is at the very back of the building, on the second storey. The door is fire-engine red, with a round hole where a deadbolt should be, and it swings open without the turn of a knob or a key, as if James is doing some elaborate squatting. Inside is a small one-room apartment with no kitchen, just a bathroom. James mentions that he took over the lease from his old drug dealer, and that the space still has a rep from back then.

"No one would wander in even if I left the door wide open. The guy who dealt out of here was an absolute monster."

The space has a wall of mirrors like a ballet studio and a wall of three windows facing out onto an unsuspecting residential street. The rest of the drywall has been painted menstrual red, and a patch of wall just inside the door is scribbled over with black Sharpie in countless sets of handwriting.

"That's the yearbook, sweetie."

The Shibari Salon is a room within a room: James has constructed a wooden suspension rig to fit the entire space, like a rib cage pushing back against the room's walls, floor, and ceiling. It's almost comical to see such a big suspension rig in such a small area, and I immediately think of it like a Surrealist Magritte painting, like a huge boulder taking up every inch of a bedroom. The timber frame of the rig is sturdy enough to support a series of thick rafters along the ceiling. Along the top inside edges, a series of women's underwear—all clearly owned and abandoned by different women—is stapled into the rig, hanging down like trophies or like Christmas decorations. The Shibari Salon is equal parts high concept, lowbrow, skeezy, and amazing.

James and I tie, and it's feral. On the floor of the Shibari Salon, we become otherworldly gremlins, growling in freedom and delight with each other.

After the scene, I lie on the tatami flooring of the space, looking up at the trophy underwear while James sits on a window ledge, smoking and staring at the sky between buildings.

"Sweetie, we're not going to have sex today," he says, breaking the post-rope silence.

He tells me there are things I need to know before I can decide if I want to incorporate sex into our friendship. He lays out his life. He tells me that while he's going to meetings and has a sponsor, for him, relapse is a very real possibility. He explains which STIs he's had, which he still has, and how he handles that with sex partners. He explains that he has a lot of sex partners, more than he can name off the top of his head, which is why he tends to call everyone sweetie. He tells me that one of his partners is a woman he is completely in love with, that she's the priority of his heart, and that that's not going to change. He explains that his residency in Canada is not permanent, and while he hopes for that to change, he can't guarantee it, so our friendship may end abruptly. He tells me that he ties for joy, but he also ties people he's not interested in, if they'll pay. He tells me that we can keep tying together for fun, without fucking, if that's what I'd like to do.

"And if you like, I would like to fuck you," he concludes.

Whereas I have a rules-of-play stump speech, James has desire and disclaimers. He's the fire I'm drawn to, even though I don't want to get burned. We don't have sex after our first tie. We do fuck nearly every time we see each other afterward, more often than we explore bondage.

We get together weekly, mostly after he teaches his last rope class of the day. I swing by the Shibari Salon around 10 p.m., when his students are petering out and the Hideaway starts blasting music downstairs. Sometimes James sends one of his students down to let me in. When he comes down himself, he always answers the door grinning, like I'm shiny and new.

He's always in a good mood and never takes my presence for granted. He never processes his drama with me, complains about anything, or asks for sympathy. He's always just hungry for body contact, hungry for fun, hungry for rope, hungry for wildness, and deeply pleased that I'm there. It's an addictive relief to have someone in my life who is always so happy to see me without wanting me to facilitate something, do something, or be something in return. It's the first time I've ever had someone treat me that way.

Over and over, I show up to the piss-soaked front of the Hideaway, and the minute I'm inside off the street, James reaches into my pants with his long callused fingers. Eventually we make it up to the Salon, trading hand jobs through the winding hallways of the building. Sometimes we tie, mostly we fuck, always we get loud, animalistic, and bleary eyed. As we come down from our play, we talk about how to get what we want out of life, sometimes in a booth at Java Joint, sometimes over bags of candy in the Salon while the Hideaway's music reverberates through the building.

Before dawn, we part ways. James climbs the stairs back to the Salon to fall asleep on an old futon while I head home in the back of a streetcar, feeling raw all over in the best way, surrounded by women in body-con dresses heading home from the clubs on King Street. As the party girls ditch their heels, massage their sore feet, and slip their bare toes through the red felt of the streetcar seats, I echo this ritual by fingering the ligature marks James's rope has left across my chest and smelling the rope dust still on my skin. At 5 a.m., the streetcars in Toronto are full of people like us, tenderly coming down from the high we've been on and licking our wounds.

I live in my imagination a lot. It's a survival mechanism I developed as a kid to give myself a mental break from the hell of my home. Well past that time, it's a habit I haven't dropped because it still gives me a break—only now it's from stressing out about rent, hating my creepy boss, fearing that I have no future, and worrying that I don't belong anywhere. The thing is, I don't live in my imagination when I'm with James. Instead, I feel present. Whether I'm sitting across from him at Java Joint at 4 a.m. swapping life stories, writing my thoughts down on his laptop while he watches *The Simpsons* next to me, or lying naked on the tatami flooring with his dick in my face, the rest of my life begins to feel like a long, very crappy dream, and being around James begins to feel like the only time I'm really awake.

Over and over, as I head home from the Shibari Salon, the club girls on the streetcar sing Rihanna's "Only Girl (In the World)" at the top of their lungs, still drunk off their asses.

Over and over, I feel so much love for the club anthems and confidence spilling out of these women, for the woman I used to be, for the gender-to-be-decided person I'm becoming, for ecstasy in whatever shape it comes, and for nights when every reality other than joy melts away.

Through this weekly ritual of rawness and rope with James, I begin to build the confidence to recalibrate who I am, how I understand myself, and how to articulate those shifts to the people around me. In queer circles, if anyone asks me what pronouns I use, I begin to say, "Any pronoun used with respect works for me."

I feel fragile recalibrating where to draw strength from when I've always drawn it from trying to be as femme as possible—even when that femininity fit me like a clown costume. For people who don't contemplate transition, it's hard to understand the weight of what it means to dip your toes into a gender role other than the one expected of you by society. When a cis woman pulls on her boyfriend's jeans, the action doesn't come with a tsunami of anxiety because there's nothing at stake. When I stand in a store in front of a wall of boxers, with cis men standing beside me, shopping with their girlfriends while I try to discretely figure out what boxer size I am, I feel like I might pass out because I know at any moment, anyone might turn and ask me, "What are *you* doing *here*?"

There are so many real threats that all trans and non-binary people face—humiliation, violence, abuse by the medical system, sexual harassment, being assumed to be a predator by people who are uncomfortable with our existence—and as I begin to transition, I begin to experience these things. But hour by hour, minute by minute, it's the pervasive hum of this high-stakes question anyone might ask me at any time ("What are you doing here?") that haunts me, because I don't have an answer.

Knowing James helps me to feel less afraid of this question, because he never makes me feel out of place. He never comments on the fact that I'm fumbling to find my own masculinity, never makes fun of the fact that I sound like Lisa Simpson but look like Bartholomew. He never judges me. He's never embarrassed by me. He always makes it clear in front of his students, colleagues, and other lovers that I'm his lover. He never acts like it matters what my gender expression might say to anyone else about his own sexuality. When I come watch him tie at BMBE, he sticks his tongue out at me from onstage, bounds over to me when the moment allows for it, and lays a sloppy, sandpaper-tongued lion kiss on my face in front of everybody.

Over and over, I show up at James's studio with my short hair, boxers, and men's T-shirts, which hang so loosely on my frame that I look like a boy whose parents are buying him clothes they assume he'll grow into. James is the first cis man I don't costume myself as a woman for. Night after night with him, I practice being myself on new terms.

He stands me in front of the mirrored wall of his rope studio and says, "Look at you. You're perfect."

As we sit in Java Joint in the wee hours of the night over post-sex pad Thai and bowls of low-quality ice cream, we talk about women we think are sexy, women James is fucking, and women I wish I were fucking—even though I'm not sure what sex means for me in the delicate origami work of refolding my sense of identity. James is always more straightforward about things than I am. He's unencumbered by self-consciousness or the expectations of society and encourages me to be the same way.

"Here's your pickup line, sweetie: 'Hi, I'm Sly.' That's all you need."

I thought James would be a straight guy I'd put up with in order to get tied more often. Instead he becomes my rope top, my lover, my wingman, the older male mentor I never had a chance to have, and my friend.

Sometimes we talk about his students. Most of them are strangers to me, but as James shares about his teaching days, one of them isn't. A surprisingly strong woman with limitless energy and a faint British accent, like she's been away from home for a long time but part of her will always be running through the rolling fields of the English countryside. He's teaching rope bondage to Evie.

James is on my mind as I sit with Evie in a dumpling house in Chinatown. Being near her, my body is full of vague desire that feels as urgent as it is unactionable. If I had a dick, it would be small and rock hard. If I were invited to put my small rock-hard dick anywhere near her, I'd bust my load in 2.5 seconds. I'm nervous. Even though I've tangentially known her for years, her presence still transforms me into the fifteen-year-old teenage boy I never was and kind of always have been.

Sitting with Evie, I summon a performance of the confidence James always told me I should have in myself, rather than any confidence that's legitimately there. I want to be what Evie wants, and even though James would say that I'm more than enough for anybody, I don't feel that way. If Evie told me to grow out my hair, put it in pigtails, and wear a schoolgirl outfit, I might do it. I know that I'm not a woman, but I'm still bad at honouring who I am in the face of what I want.

We chat about James, who she misses as a teacher and who I miss on a level that's hard to quantify. It's been a year since James's visa ran out and he left Canada. His departure has made me feel like all the lights in the city have gone dim. I haven't figured out the balance of my life in Toronto without James around. Most days it feels like I'm just going through the motions. I go to a job I hate just so I can barely afford my expenses. I go to yoga on the weekend and pretend to be invested in my wellness. I hang out with people I know and feel more alone in a room full of them than I do on my own. James had the perpetual soul of a five-year-old, and like a small kid, he addressed life with a degree of candour and wonder that made it easier for me to find the wonder in the world too. The absence of our weekly hangouts makes me feel distant from reality, not because my life is discernably worse than it was before I met James, but because now that he's gone, I can pinpoint what my life is missing. Evie doesn't have the soul of a five-year-old, but she, like James, wants a life less ordinary. Sitting with her feels like turning some of the lights back on.

"There was something very special about learning to tie from James," Evie agrees.

I look at her hands and picture her learning to tie from him. Everything about Evie is effortlessly femme except for her hands, which are coarse and wide like they've toiled in fields. The solidness of her hands feels appropriate, as if any hands James taught rope to would have to be strong in order to contain the weight of his knowledge, sensibilities, and rigour. They aren't pretty hands, but like James's, they're the hands of someone who knows what it takes to be free.

We order dumplings. Evie tells me some Japanese words and their translations. It's a thing James always used to do too. I wonder if this is something she picked up from him, if it's a coincidence that they both obsess over what they love in the same way, or if this is a tendency among all professional fetishists. Evie asks me what I do for a living. I realize that while I know a little about her, she knows next to nothing about me.

"I work in cubicle in North York doing underpaid IT for a shitty fast-fashion company, in an industrial district of damaged-goods discount outlets and stores that sell As Seen on TV products."

Evie looks at me like I've sprouted a second head. I ask her why she decided to tell me she was a professional dominatrix the first time I met her.

"I outed myself because I thought you were a sex worker."

"Why did you think that?"

"You have great breasts. You're petite. And you were walking around Feast Unleashed in three-hundred-dollar underwear."

"I buy things I can't afford because I lack self-esteem."

Evie laughs, shaking her head. "With what I do, I size people up. Annual incomes, professions—I pick up a picture quickly. I really thought you were a sex worker."

"I do a little writing and performing, but I'm mostly a broke office worker with poor impulse control and a high credit card limit."

She smiles. "I'll buy dinner this time, then, since I make three hundred an hour and you keep blowing your money on slutty underwear."

She tells me about how often she travels for work, the investment banker she met at her gym whom she's just started dating, the first husband she's finalizing her divorce from, and how she loves eating Oreo cookies at home alone while watching *Peaky Blinders*. I tell her about growing up in Montreal, about moving to Toronto when I was fourteen, and about talking my way into my IT job without any real skills at eighteen, because that was the age at which I needed to start relying on myself financially. She tells me about her childhood, which was 50 percent an idyllic countryside life of wealth and leisure when her father was away for business and 50 percent a terror when he was home. I tell her about the cycles of violence in my family, the way kink helps me metabolize those experiences, and how rope bondage helps me feel less ashamed of my shit-show personal history. It's a bizarrely honest conversation. We don't play together that night, or the next time we get together, or the time afterward. We date each other slowly. We don't jump into kink, rope, or sex right away.

The first time Evie and I play, she invites me over to the private dungeon she owns and operates. It's a very small townhouse, wedged in an alley and designed to attract minimal attention to how many cars come and go from the building as her clients arrive and depart from sessions.

Evie's dungeon is a love letter to her craft, her livelihood, and the way she sees the world. There's a glass cabinet displaying her collection of dildos and harnesses. There's a wall of sensory deprivation hoods on mannequin heads, in everything from basic black to more humiliating latex pig faces. Looking at the wall of hoods feels like looking at all the strangers, both clients and other lovers, who have worn these hoods as Evie bent them over and whaled on their asses or stretched out their sphincters. The space tells the story of a pro dom who's a pro for a reason: there's nothing casual and little off limits to the way Evie plays.

She has a human-sized dog cage tucked discreetly into the townhouse's kitchen. She has rope, whips, needles, and smaller instruments of pain and discomfort displayed. She likes things fancy and ornate as much as she likes them practical and ordinary. She has specialized items on hand such as an IV drip bag for medical play and mundane but reliable tools like duct tape—and she treats the custom and the commonplace with equal affection. The largest objects on the main floor of the space are a Saint Andrew's cross, a spanking bench, a medical examination bed, and a floor-to-ceiling mirror facing a hardpoint in the ceiling. In the loft space above, a California king–sized bed is surrounded with wall and ceiling mirrors, more hardpoints for suspension around the gigantic bed frame, and a custom neon sign that glows purply pink and says, "Yes, please."

Even the bathroom has rubber rope in it, with a hardpoint installed in the shower ceiling. The level of customization and personal taste present in Evie's dungeon makes the Shibari Salon look like a generic conference room by comparison. If you aren't into kink, her townhouse dungeon is a vision of hell. If you are into kink, her townhouse is pretty much heaven.

The first thing Evie does with me is ask me if I'd like to shower. Yes, please.

Standing in her bathroom, she undresses me, places me in the shower, and ties my arms above my head with rubber rope into the hardpoint in the shower ceiling. Then she undresses in front of me while I stand there, watching. We're naked and alone together for the first time. I've only ever seen her get kinky with an audience at Feast Unleashed or in photos on FetLife. Being alone with her, it turns out she's just as creative and detailed in her movements one-on-one as she is with an audience watching. Everything she does feels deliberate, self-assured, and full of pleasure. She steps into the shower with me, turns the water on, and slowly washes my body. She turns off the water and towels me dry while my arms dangle above me, helpless. She unties me from the hardpoint, unties my wrists, and uses the rubber rope to tie a harness around my chest with a long line at the end, like a dog leash. Then she asks me if I'd like to get down on my hands and knees.

"Yes, please."

With the rope, Evie leads me like a dog out of the bathroom; I crawl alongside her, naked and clean. She leads me to the kennel in the kitchen, squats down to untie me, opens the cage door, and asks me if I'd like to get in. The cage itself is only a little bit bigger than I am on my hands and knees, and I feel calm inside it as Evie closes the cage door and locks it with a dainty key. My thoughts begin to constrict and expand and follow a different form of logic, the way they always do as subspace kicks in.

I think about how the cage I'm in is a room within a room, just like James's suspension rig in the Shibari Salon. I think about how playing with Evie is a scene within a scene, because Evie learned to tie from James, and James used to tie me. I think about how bondage and confinement make my problems feel small. I think about how this cage is small, and I'm even smaller than the cage is, so that must mean I'm very tiny, and my problems must be microscopic. I crawl around the cage happily, like a puppy, and growl as I stop thinking in language entirely. I arch my back up toward the top of the cage, shiver from the cold bars against my spine, and feel safe. Through the bars, I can see Evie putting on underwear and a bra, moving around the space, and selecting items for whatever play she has in mind next. I can see her, but it feels like I'm watching with a soft focus, taking in details without assigning meaning to them, without expectation or worry. A happy dreaminess washes over me.

Evie kneels down by the cage, holding the dainty key, a dog bowl, and a bottle of water. She places the dog bowl on the floor inside the cage, shows me the key purposefully before placing it in the bottom of the dog bowl, and pours water into the dish.

"If you want to come out of the cage to continue our play, you can lap up all the water in this dish," she instructs me.

I yip like a dog—not like person pretending to be a dog, but like a creature whose level of delight cannot be expressed in human terms. I feel so protected in this cage and so grateful to be assigned this simple task. I don't have to be a person anymore, or be on top of things, or be getting my shit together. Instead I can be something simpler. I can be good, and doing everything I need to in life just by lapping up this water. My hands aren't tied. I could use them to pick up the dog bowl, but I don't—why would I do anything that breaks the spell of this moment? Instead I bend my front legs, point my naked puppy butt up toward the top of the cage, and lap at the water with my tongue while Evie watches. After I finish drinking, I pick up the dish with my mouth—I want to show her what a good job I've done. She takes the dish from my mouth and checks that I haven't chipped anything on the dog bowl by running her finger along the ridges of my teeth. This act of care for my well-being and the feeling that someone else will look out for me when I'm not looking out for myself fills me with trust. She unlocks the cage.

She has jute rope in her hand now instead of rubber. She beckons me out of the cage. I stay on all fours instinctively, and she invites me to climb up onto her spanking bench, face down and ass skyward. She uses the rope to tie my torso to the bench, tight, so that I'm not going anywhere. My puppy-like brain smells the earthiness of the jute and imagines running through the English countryside with her—Evie as herself, and me as a beagle, ready to follow her anywhere. Evie shows me what she's selected: two tiny silver clamps connected by a chain. She moves behind me to where my genitals are elevated and exposed and clamps one end of the chain at a time to each of my labia. She tugs lightly on the chain, and my thoughts constrict and expand again. I'm not puppy-like anymore. My eyes are wide. I'm screaming. I can feel Evie's pleasure in what I'm experiencing from the way she intermittently lets the chain slacken, then pulls at it again. The pain from the clamps digging into my labia is specific and excruciating.

She unties me, beckons me to stand up, and walks me the floor-to-ceiling mirror, now using the chain attached to my labia as a leash. The chain pulls down on the clamps so that I feel weight pulling down on my cunt in a place where I don't have weight, but I would if I'd been born with a cock instead. I look at the length of the chain hanging down in my reflection, like the outline of the cock I wasn't born with but still have on some other plane of existence. Evie looks at me with her different-coloured eyes, like she was born wearing 3-D glasses, born to see the missing dimensions in what's already there. She cups the chain in her hand and raises and lowers it so the pull on my cunt decreases and increases again. It feels like she's jerking me off. I can feel my cunt and my cock all at once. I feel like there's nothing to actualize, no question that could torpedo me, no transition to finance, and nothing to prove—I am whole, complete, and uncompromised just as I am. My cunt and my cock are both there.

It feels so fucking good.

Evie releases the clamps. She scoops me up, places me on her kitchen island, and starts finger-fucking me. She's grinning, turned on and hungry. I ejaculate all over the counter, her hands, and her arms and torso, harder than I've ever come. So hard that I start laughing and shaking. I've never ejaculated before. My body is coming in a way it's never come before. She's helped me to transform, find myself, be myself, and I've screamed, endured, and poured a lake onto her kitchen counter. She kisses me and asks if I'll spend the night with her in the California king upstairs. I am so completely hers. As I am James's. As I am my own.

Evie tells me she's going to tidy up the space. She mops up my ejaculate with paper towels, wipes down her spanking bench, and places the tiny clamps and chain in disinfectant. I sit on the counter and watch her, my chin resting on my bent knees. I think about the sequence of events, people, and connections that have occurred in order for me to be sitting naked on Evie's kitchen counter, the indentations of her ropework lining my rib cage.

Kink makes the world smaller. Because of the complexity and danger involved in practices like rope bondage, there is a level of tying at which rope is the intersection of lust, fine art skills, fine motor skills, and anatomical understanding. This combination is specific and specialized enough that there aren't that many people in the world who possess it, so it's not surprising that Evie and James, two of my riggers, know each other. In fact, it's comforting.

After a tie, the ligature marks that a rigger has left in my skin, sometimes shallow and messy, sometimes deep and distinct, have turned my body into a landscape sculpture. With rope, they've carved into my calves, arms, and torso roads toward the inner-most iteration of myself.

They've seen what I look like outside of all the societal roles I decide to play and all the ones I can't opt out of. They've given me a moment of clarity about my true nature, and I've let them see me without any artifice. James and Evie are very different people, but I feel similarly certain about who I am with both of them. I feel appreciated, brutalized, and galvanized by this lineage of lovers whose hands have learned from each other, whose sensibilities let me feel out who I really am, and whose hearts move in the same ways.

Over dumplings, Evie said that the Japanese word for having an orgasm is iku, but iku actually means to go somewhere. So, while on one continent our lovers come, on the other side of the world, our lovers go. Held in the hands of lovers who make the world feel smaller, I'm coming into myself and beginning to go somewhere new.

PISS PLAY

Water pools around me. I'm lying flat on my back in the bathtub in the small windowless washroom Max shares with her roommate. Max has placed lit candles and tea lights all over the bathroom, wedged into ledges, crevices, and anywhere there's a bit of flat space; it's a vision of Urban Outfitters–inspired Millennial gothic glamour. The dancing light of the candles bounces off the white tiles lining the room while synth-pop echoes from the sex playlist Max says she's been putting together for us all week.

Max and I are almost the same age and living the same experience of teetering toward thirty. She's a fine art handler and freelance photographer, which sounds impressive but pays poorly. I'm still working my underpaid IT job by day, and by night I'm breaking into being a writer and performer through a combination of night school classes, open mics, and self-funding my self-actualization with credit card debt. We're both at that age when our hustles have no sustainability, living paycheque to paycheque, minimum payment to minimum payment. We keep with the hustle anyway because it seems like there's nothing else to do.

Max and her roommate live above the last biker bar left in West Queen West, a neighbourhood *Vogue* magazine has just named one of the coolest places in the world to be. Max is an unapologetic, pretty mess. She's got an ongoing roster of lovers, a bunch of unprocessed trauma, an obsession with supernatural erotica, and she loves the Father of the Bride movies. She self-medicates with a combination of booze, party drugs, melted cheese on all food, and making sure that she's rarely alone. She's tall and freakishly physically strong, and she always wears floral sundresses and knee-high combat boots, no matter what the weather is. She's constantly in the process of quitting cigarettes. She's got a set of chains and wrist restraints permanently attached to her bedposts and a pirate-sized chest of sex toys at the foot of her bed. In fetish terms, she's a switch. In sexuality terms, she's pansexual. In terms of our relationship, she's my girlfriend and my dominant, and she's got a face like Kylie Minogue. She's a lot, and completely incredible. When I first met her, I liked her immediately.

I've been dating Max for a few months, very intensely—one of these queer relationships that goes from zero to a hundred based on having complementary kinks, sharing a penchant for romance, understanding each other's lived experiences really well, and very badly wanting to fuck each other.

Max is one of the least judgmental people I've ever met, which is a good and a difficult thing. The good part is that she never rejects anyone for the things they say or do. The difficult part is the same, because people take advantage of her open nature. The fact that she never sets boundaries with anyone creates a whirlwind of drama around her. She's easy to talk to but hard build a life with, because she's one of the many people who know that it's okay to not be okay but have failed to grasp that it's okay to want to be okay, too. I adore her but find the chaos of her social circle difficult to navigate, which adds to the intensity of our dynamic. We're incessantly fighting and then reconciling over daylong makeup sex sessions and junk food.

Max is naked and straddling me, leaning over me where I lie in her bathtub. Her pupils are wide and lively in the flickering candlelight. Her small breasts hang off her rib cage and whisper deep comfort to my brain the way certain breasts feel like home and let you know who you are. Hers are the kind of breasts I want to stare at and suck on until this life is over and I've gone full circle to being a baby again. There's a vein in her forehead pulsing. Her beautiful eyes are pulled taut by her smile. She hovers above me. My mouth is full of filthy words and pleas.

"Yes, please, I want it on me, make me yours, yes," I beg.

Her eyes are full of pure devil's food cake delight. The synth-pop bounces against our teeth and the bathroom tiles as we both grin. We're in a mending-things-and-fucking part of our roller-coaster relationship. We always feel open to each other, physically and emotionally, at this point in the ride. It's easy to imagine that maybe we're in love.

This is when Max pees on me. This is the first time anyone pees on me.

Her piss pours down from her crotch and pools in the bathtub water. I can feel her warm piss pouring down on my clit. I can feel her piss cascading over the lips of my cunt. I can smell her piss in the water around me. I moan and lean back into the tub, knowing there's piss against the back of my neck. There's piss in my hair. She bends down and kisses me. I'm so happy. I look up at her as she pulls back from our kiss, and I smile. I am in awe that she would give me something so intimate because I asked for it.

I've never watched or read any piss play pornography, nor even thought about looking at it. My relationship to my own urine is fraught with fear and negative associations. I get urinary tract infections constantly, almost every time I start having sex with someone new, despite taking all the safe sex precautions. Some of my UTIs have become kidney infections. Just like the number of people I've had sex with, I've lost track of the number of urinary tract infections I've had. I'm constantly annoyed that my urinary tract doesn't seem to be as sex positive as the rest of me is.

Another part of my relationship with piss has to do with high-stakes situations and performance anxiety. Although I elect to stand on stages night after night in Toronto, the moment before I walk onstage, I always feel like I'm going to piss myself—and not metaphorically speaking. Before my turn to take the mic, I can usually be found hiding in the bathroom, crouched atop a toilet with my pants around my ankles like a nervous, fluid-filled gremlin.

I remember first feeling this performance anxiety at the age of fourteen, walking into a family courtroom side by side with my lawyer in the Palais de Justice in Montreal. I stop in the doorway of the courtroom and stand there, clamping my thighs together as tightly as I can, convinced that even though I just went to the bathroom, if I take another step, I'm going to pee everywhere. My lawyer puts her hand on my back, encouraging me to walk forward. I stare down the centre aisle of the courtroom at the judge's bench and at the stern older woman sitting there in her judge's robes looking back at me. I need the judge to believe me because I don't know that I'll survive if I have to go back to the way things have been. I'm terrified. That terror hits my crotch and makes my bladder scream.

My lawyer manages to get me to take penguin steps toward the bench. The judge asks me, "Did you write your affidavit with your lawyer?"

"Yes, ma'am."

"And are all the things written in this affidavit true?"

"Yes."

"Do you want to go live with your father in Toronto instead of living with your mother in Montreal?"

"Yes."

"And you don't want to see your mother again?"

"No, I don't want to see her again."

I remember thinking, I'm going to pee right here, in front of the judge, all over my new Walmart clothes bought specifically for court today. The judge will think I'm disturbed, all my credibility will be lost, and she'll send me back to the many circles of hell that are my life in my mother's custody. My pee is going to happen, and it's going to ruin everything.

This especially felt like a possibility because I'd lost control of my bladder in public before.

About a year earlier, when I was thirteen, I began to understand that I was bisexual—I am attracted to people of the same gender as me, as well as other genders. That same year, for many months, I was constantly and aggressively bullied at school by a clique of girls in my grade.

Gay-straight alliances hadn't been invented yet, or if they had, they didn't exist at the high school I went to in Verdun, Quebec, which was an under-enrolled and under-resourced anglophone school within the publicly funded English-language school system. The borough of Verdun has gentrified now, but in the era of Y2K, it was a different place. While it had a working-class past, in the 1990s and 2000s it was a neighbourhood of high unemployment, low rents, and high prevalence of vulnerable residents needing mental health supports, many of whom were patients of the local Douglas Hospital. One of Quebec's major biker gangs hung out in the borough constantly, with guys affiliated with organized crime living in and visiting their baby mamas' homes, which peppered the duplexes and triplexes of the neighbourhood. The Royal Canadian Mounted Police were around a lot. All us Verdun kids knew which diners were money-laundering fronts and which restaurants the RCMP officers liked to eat in. It was a neighbourhood of dollar shops, payday loans, and rent-to-own furniture stores. Every grocer in the area took food stamps. Some of the kids I went to school with had a parent with a job, but most of us didn't. My family and most of the families I knew were on social assistance, living payment to payment, with at least one and sometimes two parents at home all day with nothing to do. At the same time, there was no restfulness to be found, no tranquility, no quiet. The adults with jobs came and went from their workplaces and their errands under the steely gaze of people like my mother and stepfather, who sat on our balcony for hours, surveilling the street and their own boredom, intermittently walking to the depanneur in slippers to gossip and buy milk, smokes, and lottery tickets.

Within this dreariness, there was oppression, discrimination, and disregard for human potential.

At thirteen I already had one friend who was cutting herself. At first it was lines across her upper thighs that our teachers accepted her implausible explanations for. Then she started cutting the names of boys in our class into the inside of her forearm so she could get their attention.

At thirteen I knew girls only a few years older than me who'd already had several abortions and were looking for options to miscarry because they didn't want a child but didn't feel like they could go through an abortion again.

At a parent-teacher conference, my teacher told my mom that girls in Verdun got pregnant and dropped out at sixteen, so it wasn't worth investing the time and energy in seeing girls succeed.

To derive some sense of meaning and control in these circumstances, kids assigned female at birth built toxic hierarchies of popularity among themselves, often making life much more depressing, and kids assigned male at birth either engaged in escapism by leaning into geek culture or got justifiably angry and channelled their anger into fist fights with our teachers.

All the adults employed in positions meant to support us Verdun kids, be they teachers, school administrators, nurses, social workers, doctors, or the police, were burnt out and jaded. Quebec sovereignty had just been voted on five years earlier, and regardless of the vote results, the question didn't feel settled. We all remembered when the fronts of houses across the city were papered with "Oui" and "Non" signs, yes and no, like a consent check-in crossing over into an argument—and no one acknowledged that we were all on stolen Indigenous land anyway. The majority of Verdun was francophone, and the tension between English and French speakers hung tense and heavy on the street as the fleur-de-lys flags rippled in the wind.

I didn't grow up knowing anyone who was queer, either publicly or privately. I didn't know any trans or non-binary people, and frankly, I didn't know that trans and non-binary people existed. But I did know that I stuck out without trying to—and that was an issue.

Whether it was people picking up on my queerness, the fact that I was always the physically smallest person in my grade, my acne, or my gym teachers always saying I was too slow and too weak, I didn't fit the mould, even though I wanted to. Instead, I wore second-hand church-rummage-sale clothes that were completely out of step with the times and had difficulty covering up how violent and unstable my home life was. Despite these stress factors, I got really good grades without trying, which annoyed my AFAB cohort, who were all being abandoned by the system. I tended to be confident speaking my mind, which in the circumstances came across as arrogant. School was my daily escape from home, so I was often in a good mood in class. I needed to be in a good mood somewhere. This all made me come across as a teacher's pet, a narc, a nerd and culminated in a period of months where, instead of being my reprieve, school was just as shitty as home.

It starts with a day where I'm pelted with food in the cafeteria while people laugh and scream, like a scene that didn't make the final cut of *Heathers*. I go to the bathroom to try to clean the food and chocolate milk out of my hair, but I am followed into the bathroom and further pelted with drinks until I'm soaked to the skin. The school sends me home. My normal tactic is to hide problems from my mom because telling her that I have problems tends to make them much worse, but I don't have any money, so I can't buy new clothes to change into on my way home. My mom loses her shit. She likes a cause to be indignant about—it gives her something to do—so she calls the school, the school board, and the police, even though I just want to live it down. She stirs up such a frenzy that I return to school branded the kid who ran home to cry to mommy. A clique of girls in my grade seizes on this for months—having a common enemy bolsters group cohesion. I can't go near the cafeteria or the bathrooms without being bullied, so I hide in the library at lunchtime, stop eating food during the day, and stop going to the bathroom during school hours.

During my lunchtimes hiding out in the library, I go on the school computer, which is the only access I have to the internet. The beginnings of social media are taking shape. I set up a profile without the good sense to conceal my assigned gender or my age, so I mostly get online messages from adult cis men. They are so interested in me—where I am, what I'm doing, how developed my body is, and what kind of boys I'm interested in. It's gross, and in a lot of ways it's my escapism, so I sit at the school computer day after day, hungry, holding in my pee, and flirting with internet creeps.

One of the days in class that girls are invading my space and stealing my stuff, I get mad. I push one of them away from me and lose control of all the pee I've been holding in. I realize I can't change what's happened and wait in terror to be discovered. I'm already getting made fun of so much that I can't imagine how bad it's going to get when someone realizes that I've pissed myself, at the age of thirteen, in a classroom full of my enemies.

Somehow, no one sees.

I get through the rest of the school day without anyone noticing my wet pants or the smell. I walk home, taking deserted laneways wherever I can. My anxiety, isolation, and humiliation are private but nonetheless clinging to my legs in the cold Montreal winter air.

Piss play is one of those practices that's still taboo among folks who describe themselves as kinky. I've talked to many BDSM lifestylers who think piss play is disgusting, a thing one would only engage in for money, as in piss play for pay.

At public BDSM events and play parties, piss play and its sister, scat play, are often among the only activities that are banned. Sometimes these parties say the banning is not a judgment on proclivities but a practical matter of health and safety. A lot of those same parties are sex friendly and allow needle play, cutting, and blood play, even though blood and come are just as big a health and safety concern as piss and shit. What's more, these same events don't bat an eye at bondage or rope suspensions, when it's very easy to sustain a nerve injury hanging in rope.

In contrast to a lot of kink practices with an accepted degree of risk, being peed on is pretty physically safe, but most kinksters don't think it's sexy. What's welcome in kink communities is often determined by popular opinion rather than by critical thought and understanding.

When Max tells me that she used to pee on a former partner of hers and really enjoyed it, it clicks a light on for me in a way I never anticipated.

"Would you be interested in peeing on me?" I ask.

One of the reasons I explore kink is because it's a form of alchemy. Through kink I get an opportunity to transform experiences that are threatening into an expression of ecstasy.

Max talks about piss play with such affection. I'm no longer that kid afraid they might pee in court, but I'm still scared of my bladder and the next time my body's natural reactions might turn me into an outcast or damage my reputation. Beyond the general stigma that piss is dirty and that only babies pee themselves, piss is a manifestation of my sense of shame. Having piss play described to me as fun sex play makes me realize that the practice might allow me transform my association with piss from shame to something kinder.

"Piss play usually isn't the whole encounter. It's usually the foreplay to having sex, or age play, or a spanking scene, or all of the above." Max smiles as she takes a drag on a joint and hands it to me. "When your lover is holding your pee in the palm of their hand, you know that you're accepted as you are. There's no thinking that you're not hot enough. There's no lingering internalized bullshit about being queer tugging at the corners of your brain. There's no idea of yourself that you're trying to present. You're good."

"The last time we were comfortable pissing in another human's arms was when we were infants and toddlers. When we were creatures without apology, in a time before embarrassment or dread," I respond.

"Yep. You're getting it."

"Yes, please, I want it on me, make me yours, yes," I beg.

Max's piss feels warm as it hits my clit and trickles over my labia—so much warmer than I expect it to be, and delicate. Rather than overwhelming the nerve endings in my clit the way faucet water or skin-on-skin stimulation does, this feels like just the right warmth, intensity, and friction. Her piss feels like what I expect I'm supposed to feel when people lick my clit but don't because direct contact on my clit feels mushy, hard, imprecise, and numbing.

It's not that I can't come hard: I just need the right sensory input and psychological circumstance to come hard.

The physical sensation of her piss works for me—it really works for me—and that makes me feel safe.

I begin to breathe hard, even though I feel at ease. I close my eyes. From behind my eyelids, I see the hard edges of life— the edges of objects, the delineations between then and now— beginning to soften and blur into a comforting haze. Now I'm in Max's candlelit bathroom, but I'm also in my childhood bath- room in Verdun. Now I can feel the girls I knew when I was thirteen jabbing at my body, but I can also feel the warmth of Max's body over mine. Now I can hear the pages of my affidavit turning in the judge's hands and feel like I'm going to pee all over the place—but I also know that I can let go, I can unclench, I can pee everywhere in this bathtub if I need to, and nothing bad is going to happen. Everything I am and have been is allowed.

I lean back into the piss and bathwater in the tub. Max looks down at me, scoops up a handful of piss and bathwater in her hand, and pours it gently over my tummy. It feels soft, familiar, and loving, like an inside joke and a hug simultaneously. I feel secure and tended to. I begin to slip into the headspace of being a little.

Max is tall, stronger than me, and caring for me. I feel like a child in a plastic wash basin, looking up at her. I feel the delight of freedom of movement in my pudgy thighs and toothless mouth. Our piss play creates a context for comfortable vulnerability and sensation, and the vulnerability and sensation become a mechanism of time travel and cross-dimensional exploration.

Now I'm myself, but from a different place in the multiverse, a me that had a loving childhood. Max slowly pours piss and bathwater into my belly button, over my knees, and into my armpits, where it tickles. Her soft palmfuls of piss, her kindness, and the synth-pop work to gently rearrange history. I feel okay with where I've been, the things I've been through, and what they mean to me. It's not a feeling of forgiveness. It's a feeling of the past hurting less than it used to because the past has been added to, the context has been widened, and the experiences have had joy and care added into the mix.

Max and I look at each other in the candlelight, hanging in this timeless moment.

This healing feels like an energetic potential in me, and I feel shock waves emanating from me like techno beats, but I don't speak—I wouldn't do anything that breaks the spell of this moment. Max doesn't ask me to say anything.

She scoops up my head, sits me forward in the bathtub, and pulls up the stopper. The bathwater and piss whirlpool at the far end of the tub, between my little feet. I watch it, fascinated, like I've never seen a bathtub drain before. I splash my palms in the shallowing water. Max turns the faucet on and holds the inside of her wrist under the tap to make sure the fresh water is the right temperature. She gets a washcloth, soaps it, and gently runs the soapy washcloth through my hair, around my neck, over my shoulders, and up and down my outstretched arms while I hold tight to her biceps. My fingertips push into her skin of her arms, like digging into sand on the beach. I'm fascinated by the landscape of her body. Even the give of her skin under my fingers seems miraculous.

She stands me up so that we're toe to toe and pulls the shower curtain closed around us. Now the world, is even smaller. The candlelight is dimmed by our plastic cocoon. I feel shy without feeling uncomfortable, staring at her blood-red toenail polish. She turns on the shower head and carefully runs her finger pads through my short hair, while soap suds flow down my back and pool, forming the tiniest bubbles, between her toes. She steps back from me. I watch her soap and rinse her own cunt. It feels like I'm in the changing room of a public pool, suddenly. Watching her wash herself feels raw and open and like I'm allowed to see because there's nothing wrong with being naked, but at the same time, like this is something I only get to see in this specific social situation—so I drink in the details. I watch the way soap sticks to her pubic hair. I look at the way her powerful legs hinge into her hips. I look at the soft and delicate ripples of cellulite at the outer edges of her frame, where her thighs meet her butt cheeks. She's the most gorgeous being I've ever seen.

She steps out of the bathtub, gets a towel, and dries me off. I keep feeling like a brand-new wide-eyed creature, because Max nurtures me and lets me stay in that headspace. She wraps the terry cloth around me so her roommate won't see me naked. She tells me to run to her bedroom and climb into her bed. I scamper to her bed gleefully; I feel like her instruction has let me discover what my feet are for.

Max follows me in, and the playlist from the bathroom continues in her bedroom. Electric Youth's "The Best Thing" comes on, and I recognize the song without remembering the name of the band or the album title. As I look at Max, I feel the song's feeling. I watch her move around the room and mouth along to the song's lyrics.

She closes her bedroom door, lets her towel drop to the floor, and unwraps mine. I'm all eyes and quiet. She asks me to lie down and roll onto my stomach. I do. She opens her pirate chest of sex toys and pulls out a butt plug. She shows it to me, and I nod yes. This is our consent code, especially when I'm in a headspace better maintained by being non-verbal: she'll show me the toy she has in mind, and I can shake my head, or nod if I want it. I want it.

She lubes my sphincter with her fingers, slowly and softly, with the same kind of patience as when she was washing my hair. She takes her time stuffing the butt plug into my asshole.

"Loosen and the squeeze your butt muscles around the butt plug."

"I don't know how to do that," I answer.

Usually I'm embarrassed when lovers ask me to localize and control muscles in my body because I don't know how, and it feels a little like disappointing a gym teacher again, as though everyone else attained a level of coordination and agility while I wasn't around, and now I don't fit in. With Max, though, I'm not embarrassed. I accidentally squeeze the butt plug out of my ass completely. Max smiles. She's not annoyed or impatient.

"You're good," she responds, as she slowly pushes the butt plug back in.

Max returns to the pirate chest. I stay on my stomach and swirl my fingers around the nub of the butt plug still protruding from me while I watch Max step into the harness lines of her strap-on.

"Pirate booty for my booty," I say, flicking the nub and feeling the plug move inside me.

Max looks up from tightening her harness around her hips, the goofiest grin on her face.

"You did not just fucking say that."

"It's booty for my booty."

"I fucking cannot with you."

It's the kind of stupid dad joke that I knew would make her smile. I really like making her smile. She carries such complicated histories in her past, and I want to see her happy.

She lies down on her back beside me in her strap-on. Her small breasts melt into her chest. Her slender black-silicone cock sticks straight up at the ceiling.

"All right, climb up here and ride Daddy," she says. "Daddy's going to fill all your holes."

I ride my girlfriend's cock. I am healed and made new, over and over, in the tension of her squeezed-shut eyes, in the stretch of her long neck against her bed, and in the corners of her wide open, cigarette-stained mouth. I live for any fluids she wants to give me. I watch her come and feel so comfortable with everything that's made me who I am, while my piss-stained cunt grinds her dick.

The next day, I sit in my cubicle in North York, completely unharmed but weighed down and heartbroken at having to return to the dreariness of my office job so soon after being in such an elevated state of joy, compassion, and self-acceptance. In this workplace, I'm back at my Montreal school, hiding in the library on lunch breaks.

Between night classes, open mics, the polyamory I'm engaged in, and working fifty hours a week, I might be getting comfortable with my past, but I'm also exhausted.

It feels like even though my lawyer and I got me out of Montreal and set in motion the very different life I'm living now, I'm struggling. Now the struggle is trying to squeeze moments of myself into the cracks between my obligations and ambitions and hoping that my hard grind will pay off at some point, because I'm not really building stable partnerships, resting, or making enough money.

I'm grateful for my night of piss play with Max and the authenticity of the experience. Now that the piss play is over, the drop is profound and gutting. I want to cry as I look at the Tupperware container of lunch sitting on my desk that Max packed for me this morning.

I quietly tear up, move my mouse around the screen when I feel someone walking past my cubicle, blast Electric Youth in my earbuds, and make up mediocre poetry.

> She is the river that wears down stone and
> makes new caves in my body
> For me to crawl into and laugh and splash in
> In the warm and wet and small places where
> there is no shame

Max and I keep dating, and the unsustainable volatility doesn't change.

In the lulls between our issues—Max's friends trying to hook up with her on our dates, Max showing up to my work drunk and belligerent, Max assuming she can fix our problems by asking me to marry her—we talk about our pasts. The volatility of our romance sucks because we aren't on the same page about what love looks like, but in a lot of other ways, Max and I are on exactly the same page.

On one of my nights at Java Joint with James, I ask him why Max would propose we get married when we can't even get through a week without fighting.

"Aw sweetie, I've done that. A woman I was seeing before I left Tokyo. I was just afraid to lose her."

Through the fetish Max and I explore and through our conversations, I come to believe that I shouldn't blame myself or feel shame over the places where I've found comfort and pleasure when I was trapped, isolated, desperate, and sitting at school library computers. In those moments of being really alone, anything that made me feel connected to the world, valuable, or connected to myself was a benefit.

I begin to look at shame as a signpost, instead of a location I live in; shame points to the situations I don't ever want to be in again and the things I don't ever want to do again. By reclaiming moments of pain and humiliation through my play with Max, my past stops feeling like a secret I'm dragging around with me, destined to feel heavy or destined to be repeated.

Max and I break up, even though our differences are smaller than what we have in common.

My writing in night school classes gets more candid, and at open mics across the city I begin letting it all hang out onstage— the good, the bad, what's piss-soaked, and where I find peace.

F TO X,
NOT F TO M

I want you to bring your harness, Kyle texts me.

I've moved from Toronto to the postcard city of Vancouver, to be part of a place that's formed by its stark contrasts. The beauty of its pristine waterways and snow-capped peaks is undermined by the gutting financial poverty and associated social problems created by high real estate prices. My career as a Canadian theatre professional has taken off, in the form of being awarded an eight-month paid artist residency in Vancouver. This means that I'm making less than minimum wage now, every day is like going into combat against calamity, and I'm still going into credit card debt every month—but I'm not working in IT in Toronto anymore. Instead, I'm short-term employed as an honest-to-God artist in this mountain-lined metropolis and travelling around Canada to perform. I settle into a cockroach-infested 250-square-foot shithole on the edge of Vancouver's Downtown Eastside. I live above a dilapidated nightclub called Now and Always. My one window overlooks the alley beside the club, where DTES residents scream their justified rage into the night and kids from

Abbotsford do coke off the top of and then have sex against the club's dumpsters. The kids in from out of town who end up at Now and Always don't have a lot of money and come for the five-dollar drinks on their big night in the big city. In Vancouver I'm worried about cash flow and confronted by the agony of existence all the time, but I don't cry at my desk anymore. When I post on Facebook, I say I'm living the dream.

I've been on the road for work for five weeks, so it's been five weeks since Kyle and I had our third date. From his Vancity Yaletown apartment, Kyle texts me GIFs he's made of his own juicy ass bouncing up and down in a thong. I jerk off to his juicy ass GIFs as a matter of principle; when you've just started seeing someone and they send you nudes, jerking off to their nudes is the polite thing to do. I send Kyle flattering photos of my sun-soaked naked body from the homes of friends and artist billets across the country and get back OMGs from him with a string of Ms in the middle.

Kyle is a queer person of stark contrasts. His sense of self seems to sit on a knife's edge. He's in his late twenties and makes good money as a structural engineer. The cost of rent in Vancouver is a form of shitty sorcery no one asked for, transforming even good money into okay money, like if Carrot Top had a Vegas magic show where he just steals your life savings. But given that Kyle's doing okay, he's one of the only Vancouverites I know who isn't running side hustles all the time, so he has time for hobbies. He lives alone and has a squad he's been rolling with since university. He's outgrown his squad but hasn't moved on from them, and he deals with the alienation he feels through a combination of hanging out with his toxic ex-girlfriends, tweeting craft beer rankings, and working out with his personal trainer constantly.

When he lets himself be more like himself, he programs Arduino, builds virtual reality environments, and makes short-form solo porn, which he posts to the internet for free and from which he earns no tips. The GIFs he sends me aren't made especially for me; they're seen by the thousands of people who follow the threads he posts to on Reddit. His solo internet porn career is an act of decompression and resilience against the person he's been conditioned to be, because he was assigned a male gender at birth. In his GIFs he does his makeup the way he'd like to, blooms like a cherry blossom in Sailor Moon costumes, and rides dildos, ass out to his cellphone screen, in flouncy American Apparel skirts. Society has conditioned him to chase the thirst trap, but he finds himself and his femme in being the thirst trap. It's both lovely and difficult to watch—lovely because he's freer in his GIFs than he is in society, and difficult because the comment threads on his posts treat him like a shameful sissy who wants to be abused. When I used to sit in the school library letting internet creeps talk down to me so at least I wasn't alone, I felt deep despair and like my escapism came at an unsustainable cost. That despair I've felt recognizes the despair in Kyle, despite his whip-smart brain, Colgate ad smile, and career that has a future to it. He's reading Japanese manga by Nagata Kabi and sees himself in the gutting panels of *My Lesbian Experience with Loneliness*. The more I text chat with Kyle while I'm on the road, the more I wish we'd gotten to be friends when we were kids.

I still date bisexual people like Kyle. I've stopped dating straight cishet dudes. My Tinder profile reads, "My looks are masc of centre. I'm non-binary. My pronouns are they/them. I only fuck queer people."

Toward the end of my days in Toronto, I'd still been telling people they could use any pronoun said with respect—but that just meant almost everyone referred to me as a woman. As I moved across the country, I decided that I deserved more than what some doctor saw when I was born. I began defining myself as non-binary and trans interchangeably, with trans being a broader umbrella term and non-binary being the term that spoke to my gender more explicitly.

In some ways, being trans or non-binary in Vancouver is easier than in the Greater Toronto Area, because in Toronto circles both straight and gay, bisexuality still faces stigma. The majority of straight and gay people in Toronto define their place in society by who they sleep with, which makes trans and non-binary folks destabilizing. While sexual orientation and gender identity aren't the same thing, often, people's hang-ups around sexual orientation inform their hang-ups about gender. The exception to Toronto's tendency to shun bisexuals is in its kink community, which is why, beyond my own tastes and turn-ons, I'd go to places like Fountain and Feast Unleashed or hang out with James and Evie—it gave me a break from bisexuality being an issue.

In the Vancouver area, I meet more openly bisexual people, most of them not too fussed about how I define my gender because my gender doesn't impact how they view their own sexuality. I also notice that none of the bisexual folk I'm meeting from New West, Po Co, Port Moody, and even farther out from the city centre seem to hang out at queer events or spaces.

This is why, on the other hand, being trans or non-binary in Vancouver is the worst. This city is the stronghold of the Canadian trans-exclusionary radical feminism movement—with Canada's most famous and accomplished TERF holding a degree in Women's Studies from Simon Fraser University.

As I get to know the city and its queer communities more, I find that the tendrils of TERF politics are everywhere in Vancouver—in the city's Dyke March, in its arts and culture organizations, and in its prominent icons and authors. Even Sam, my one-night stand and one-time dom, is part of a creepy, TERF-informed queer reading group.

I get the sense that in Vancouver, women involved in queer events might have sex with me and might dom me, but if I disappoint them or dump them, my gender will be weaponized against me. It's something I saw shades of in Sam when, after I asked to cut off contact, she messaged that if I didn't give her attention, I was using my male privilege against her. After living in Vancouver for some time, Sam's misguided understanding of my gender and her comfort in using anyone's trans identity as leverage made more sense to me, because I could see how her hometown sensibilities were shaping her.

A few months after moving to Vancouver, I'm hungry for sex, grounding, and connection, but I'm also beginning to spiral into work and income burnout, so I take a break from queer spaces and community. I don't have the spoons to sift through the complex matrix of queer culture as it exists in my new home, and honestly, only the Wachowski sisters would have the skills to make that matrix entertaining.

Before I refocus my Tinder profile, I start dating a lot of self-labelled straight cisgender men. Nice, open-minded British Columbian guys into making money, wellness culture, getting booked for TV commercials, and brewing kombucha from the SCOBY they've been nurturing.

I tell these straight guys my pronouns, they use my pronouns correctly, and I feel a huge sense of accomplishment. In and of itself, that's more than I get from most people. It takes me a while to realize that these straight guys are using my pronouns correctly because it gives them access to putting their cocks inside me, not because they understand me to be a person who has a cock too. None of them shows an interest in the cock I fuck with, nor my soft cock-and-balls packer.

I trampoline between these straight guys. They can all cope with knowing that my cock exists, as long as it's abstract. They think of my cock as a sex toy rather than a part of me, and even more so as a sex toy I use only with cis women. They don't even contemplate the reality of trans-on-trans sex—not because they'd have a problem with it, but because they're so nervous about making sure they say the right things, their social anxiety eats up the energy they could spend on actually expanding their world view. In their relationships and play sessions with me, they use the right words, but the words hold no meaning. We fuck, I moan, and the straight guys make polite sounds like "they" and "them" in return. We're just making sounds at each other.

The last of the straight cisgender men I set up a date with is the socially conscious head of a social justice NGO, and his name is Justin. He has a very typical straight-guy Tinder profile. He's in his forties, incredibly handsome, and a great dresser, someone who has mastered the art of using different pieces to take an outfit from the beach to the boardroom. His profile has a photo of him in a leather jacket on a Harley-Davidson motorcycle, which is sort of the straight BC equivalent of posing with a tiger. He's a published author. His profile subtly points out that he makes a lot of money. I still haven't found the sex, grounding, connection, or financial security that I'm looking for—and for some reason, Justin sends a Super Like my way—so I figure that at least I'll let a rich guy buy me a drink.

In some ways, Justin is exactly what I expect, and in other ways, he's enigmatic.

He's smaller in person, slight, and smooth and playful in his body movements, like a jazz lounge singer. His dark eyes twinkle. He does not own or know how to ride any kind of motorcycle. He came to work at an NGO through the pipeline of working in politics, and he got into politics through joining the BC Young Liberals for a sense of belonging when he was just a latchkey kid. He fell in love with his ex-wife because of the passion in their first kiss on their first date, then made the misguided choice to try to build a life based on a fleeting moment. His childhood was very rough. He's pulled himself up from nothing. He smokes a lot of weed. He sees and hates how broken the current government systems are but also likes meeting people like Mayor Gregor Robertson and mattering in the eyes of the establishment, no matter how broken it is. By calling himself a published author, he means that he wrote ideas on Post-its, hired a ghostwriter out of pocket, and self-published a book of his ideas, as expressed by someone else. His dreams include going to the Shambhala Music Festival in an RV and hosting an orgy in the sleeper section. He has no thoughts on the stories about Shambhala being a hotbed of self-labelled hippies engaging in cultural appropriation.

"I love love, music, romance, and excitement," he offers.

Whereas James could be straightforward about how to live in the world because he lived on the fringes of society anyway, Justin tends to oversimplify the world as a well-honed defence mechanism. In politics and outside of it, he has seen violence, cronyism, and corruption too closely and too often. He pours that knowledge into the work he does in the world of NGOs, and the rest of the time, he needs to turn his head 180 degrees away from it. If he didn't, all he'd feel is anger.

"I don't get the impression that this will be an issue for you, but I'm a Scorpio. I'm dating multiple people casually. Some are women, and some are men," Justin says, on our first date.

"Your profile comes across very straight. Why are you being so stealthy?"

"Can't a girl have some secrets?" He grins, offering his hand, palm up, across the table for me to slide my hand into.

In another place and time in my life, I wouldn't date Justin. He's charming and welcoming, but he's comfortable living in a state of cognitive dissonance between what his experiences tell him about the world and what he wants to believe. Even on our first date I know that I'm going to get frustrated. He might be a Scorpio, but I'm an Aquarius. However, in this place and time in my life, I do start dating him, because he's charming, welcoming, sexy, queer, and I need something to hang on to.

When I decided to move away from Toronto and from the Toronto kink community, I didn't feel sad about what I was leaving behind. It was too bad I wouldn't get to play with Evie as often—we still play when we're in the same city—but that was about it. Toronto was becoming financially unlivable, and while Vancouver was even more expensive, at least in BC I had a funded arts job I could count on for a bit. A lot of the long-standing Toronto institutions that we all loved—Honest Ed's, Java Joint, Suspect Video—were starting to close, and in Toronto kink circles, I saw shit go bad fast and watched a group of rope enthusiasts who called themselves a rope community stand by and do nothing to protect their community members.

Disillusioned by Toronto and becoming panicked by my new hometown of Vancouver, Justin's open palm sliding across the table to me happens to be the gesture I need. I begin a relationship based on a fleeting moment.

Once you start dating someone in Vancouver, you don't really go out on dates with them anymore. It's too cold, it rains too much, everything's too expensive, and the city's too difficult to get around without a car. Like most Vancouver couples, Justin and I dash outside to pick up Chinese takeout ordered in bulk so we can eat it all week. We restock on pre-rolled joints and run out to grab megapacks of toilet paper. Then, we spend days at a time hiding from the rain. We gravitate between sleeping, eating chili noodles with the fridge door open, and giving each other hand jobs while watching Netflix. It's comforting.

One of the days I'm headed to Justin's for some hibernation, I decide to wear my packer. The fact that I'm headed to Justin's is not part of my decision making; I'm just tired of not wearing my packer, period. On the jostling bus ride to his place, strangers give me elevator looks. Their eyes widen at the very slight bulge in my pants and then they physically move away from me. The people who have kids in tow move their kids away from me too, as if I've trespassed on their children's innocence just by sitting there.

Between the fact that strangers feel the right to look me over at all, then to shun me and behave like I'm a predator—never mind how terrible the suspension on Vancouver buses is—I get off the bus ready to vomit.

I'm just a resident of this city like anyone else, paying bus fare, going on errands, and making my way as best as I can. I'm beyond pissed that unless I present like a woman, I'm viewed as a creep and a freak before I do anything or utter a word. Life is hard enough in Vancouver, the most expensive city in the country, without cis people making trans people feel like we shouldn't be seen or heard.

I arrive at Justin's door with my eyes full of tears and rage. We hug hello. Justin doesn't notice what I'm feeling. Instead, he feels the soft bulge of my cock against his thigh.

"Did you wear that hoping I'd notice?" he asks coyly.

I stand there broken, while Justin thinks I'm introducing a new form of role play.

"No. This isn't a game I'm playing with you. This is just my life. This is just me."

Justin knows that I'm non-binary and knows that enbyphobia exists, but he never seems to expect to witness me in pain. He knows the score but misses the point.

Because he misses the point, he decides now is the moment to share with me that he's told Laura, his thirtysomething cisgender girlfriend, about me and our budding romance.

"Did you know that people think I'm non-binary?" Laura tells Justin. "They check in about my pronouns. I read as non-binary. And I think it's flattering."

Justin relays this anecdote, thinking it will have a positive impact on my brokenness.

"Dude, seriously, shut the fuck up? Please."

That night Justin and I decide to have sex, regardless of the tension in the air.

I approach our sex like an act of decompression and resilience. I fuck passionately, with the whole of my non-binary self. Justin doesn't comprehend the tensions I live within—of feeling like I can either be myself and be treated like I've committed a crime, or hide who I am and resent every trans person who is more out than me. He doesn't get that having to endure cis people who think they "get it" because they're tall, thin, and androgynous is just the icing on the cake. He doesn't understand how suffocated I feel, but maybe, through the way I fuck, he will understand my overlapping realities kinesthetically, even if he can't put that understanding into words.

I lie Justin on his stomach on his bed, while the soft glow of the Netflix menu lights up the pores along the back of his legs, the creases of his knees, and the soft patch of body hair between his shoulder blades. He's naked. I'm in my packing boxers. I push my soft packing cock all over his body like a delicate paintbrush: up and down his spine, along the edges of his ass, and between his ass cheeks. I crawl up and down his body, softly pressing into him with my soft cock, everywhere. I pull the head of my cock out of my boxers and touch it to the small concave curvature at the top of his spine. It's something James used to do to me—running his cock along the back of my neck—and it always felt unusual in a good way: feral, silly, and real.

Justin smiles into his pillow. I ask him to roll over. I poke the head of my cock out of my waistband again and touch the head of his cock with the head of mine. The pigment of his cock is darker. My cock's close to the same beige as my skin. In the dim light of the TV screen, and in the eyes of anyone wise enough to see what matters, flesh cocks and silicone cocks look exactly the same.

My packer and my fuck cock aren't sex toys to me, the way Justin's cock isn't a sex toy to him. These are just our bodies.

I feel a profound sense of grounding clarity: this is just my body.

All the blood drains out of my brain and flows directly into my swollen genitals. I roll Justin onto his face again so that I have unfettered access to his asshole.

Usually in vanilla sex, my brain's going a mile a minute—and not in a fun way—because I've never really gotten off on vanilla sex, and I've always known that I'm supposed to. Right now, even though there's no rope, clamps, or dripping hot candle wax in the mix, I'm present in the vanilla sex Justin and I are having. My mind is so quiet you could hear a pin drop in my skull. I'm out of my head and in my body because I'm having sex in my real body. It's a turn on to really be who you are.

I place my packing cock between my abdomen and the waistband of my boxers again so that it feels like my erection is pinned against me. I nestle in between Justin's outstretched legs. I eat out his asshole for a long time, him lying there, mewing, purring, and me with my hard-on physicalized and my tongue buried between his ass cheeks. I'm all top and he's all bottom, though not in a fetish sense. I have a lot to give and a lot I want to give, so I'm the top. He's the bottom because all he needs to do is enjoy and receive.

I'm usually a bottom during vanilla sex because I'm too fatigued by the searching I have to do within myself to make the sex work for me at all. To be able to enjoy the experience, often I'm miles away, reaching into the recesses of my imagination for another layer to superimpose onto the situation that's happening: a role play scenario, another place in the world, another reality where my lover is someone other than who they are and I'm someone other than who I am too. In vanilla sex, if I come, it usually has more to do with a power play dynamic I'm pretend-ing on my own, in my mind, rather than the angle of someone's finger inside me. My internal experience of vanilla sex is often a frantic one, with me flipping through a mental Rolodex of the sexual scenarios that turn me on as fast as I can so that I'm able to come before the person who's trying to make me come gets disappointed.

I'm not a bottom as I eat out Justin's ass. I have more physical energy to pour into our sex because I'm here in the moment, instead of miles away. I feel existentially whole in my physicality in a way that I usually need to sustain bruises and abrasions to get to. Justin notices the energetic difference. The words I say to him have more weight, confidence, and brevity than usual. I'm quieter—there's no nervous chatter coming out of me. I'm happier. After what feels like hours of breathing Justin in and rimming him with my tongue, his sphincter convulsing constantly, I spoon him. He rolls onto his side. I tuck his soft, tiny bum up against my packing cock again.

I spoon Justin for his benefit rather than my own. I don't really need to cuddle—even though cuddling is genuinely awesome. I've expressed my real gender in sex, I've enjoyed it, Justin's enjoyed it, and I feel at peace. I don't give a shit at this moment how people in the world read me or process who I am. I am trans. I am non-binary. I'm not in transition, pre-transition, or post-transition. I don't need to hold anyone or be held on to. I'm just me.

"Your voice sounds different," Justin says, twisting his head back to look at me.

"What do you mean?"

"Say something."

I think of James sitting in the diner booth across from me.

"Hi, I'm Sly."

"You just sound different," Justin says, as he turns away.

He drifts off. It's the first time I've used the pickup line James offered me. While Justin sleeps, I look out his bedroom window and watch a fir tree bending but standing strong in the rain and the wind.

The way I'm beginning to express my gender is some of me at my strongest, but it's also me at my frailest. Whether it's being avoided in public, seeing transphobia in people I used to have respect for, or being harassed on the street for having breasts and dark leg hair, I keep bending in the rain and the wind. Every time I bend, I wonder when will come the time I'll break because there are so many questions I don't have answers to.

Will I survive? Will I get the medical care I need? Will I become a financial and emotional burden to those around me? Will I become homeless? Will I go back into the closet? Will I detransition? Will I be able to get through airport security, buying a bottle of wine, or applying for jobs without having to explain my gender? Will I be asked if my gender is a manifestation of my trauma? Will I be asked if I'm trans because I've been abused? Will I be told that if I wear my packer outside my home, I'm sexualizing spaces? If I'm assaulted in the future, will I be told that by being obviously trans, I was painting a target on my own back? How many pat-downs, inquisitions, and well-intentioned acts of harm do I have it in me to get through? How much patience can I cultivate for when friends, lovers, and co-workers act like the fact I'm trans makes *their* lives harder? How often can I choose my battles? How many times can I walk away? How can I keep my own palms open when the world keeps folding them into fists? How often can I withstand hearing that I looked hotter before I started wearing things that are gender-affirming? How often can I be told that it's okay that I'm a boy on the streets because it makes my tits and cunt a sexy secret? What will be left of my capacity to feel love, joy, and wonder? When can I be non-binary without having to talk about it?

These are the questions that cis women like Laura don't feel the weight of or understand when she's "flattered" by being asked to confirm her pronouns.

These are the questions cis men like James can't help me through, even though James gave me the confidence to begin facing these questions.

These are the questions that queer guys like Justin can't answer with a love for love—because life is more complex than romance and infatuation.

Laura becomes a prominent topic during my days of takeout and hand jobs with Justin because she keeps insisting that she wants to meet me, and he keeps bringing it up.

It's a thing that partners often want, and she's been Justin's partner for a while, even though he says their relationship is more circumstantial than a matter of depth; the two of them have complementary work schedules. It's a very Vancouver way to approach romance, as the city squeezes everyone logistically, but I have no plans to sit through an awkward and probably degrading meal with Laura just so Justin can stop hearing her complain.

Laura's unused to the idea of a trans person saying no to her, and she can't handle it. She goes hard as a motherfucker stalking my social media, leaving comments on anything of mine that she can find that's public. She makes it very clear that her under-standing of consent only goes as far as getting what she wants, because I've already very clearly said no to contact with her.

I feel like I'm on an episode of *Maury*. I've got my Jordans on, and I'm ready to go. I'm super happy to run off-screen, off the sound stage, off the studio lot, and off into the distance where I won't be found, even for a "Where Are They Now?" clip show.

Metamour drama is not my thing.

Justin cuts Laura out of the picture, asks me to kick off my kicks, and promises things will be calm and fun if I stick around.

My relationship with Justin gets more meaningful.

In the privacy of his home, and slowly at fetish events around the city, Justin starts exploring his own gender fluidity through wigs, silk slips, and ornate nipple tassels that we source from stores targeted at rich housewives and the burlesque community.

We argue about music. He unironically loves Weird Al Yankovic, including his non-spoof acoustic stuff. He cannot convince me to get into it. I keep trying to convince him that Chance the Rapper's music is what optimism sounds like, but Justin can't stand the song arrangements.

We go on trips together. We walk the streets of foreign cities, eating too much cured meat and hitting the clubs, where European queers ask us, "Your Prime Minister Trudeau, he's gay, yes?" We go window shopping for men's clothing together, and Justin, who has had the benefit of being socialized as a man his whole life, gives me fashion lessons I can't afford to implement—but I enjoy learning just the same.

"A button-up with a blazer, slacks, and tie is business. You lose the tie, it's still business but cooler, more easygoing. You swap the button-up for a polo under a blazer, now you're headed toward business casual and weeknight date. You swap the slacks for jeans with a polo and blazer, now you're hitting the market on the weekend and getting very good customer service."

"And where does your love of Crocs fit into this equation?"

"Crocs are magic, and I can't imagine what you're trying to say." He smirks. "I'm getting you Crocs for Christmas. You just wait and see, mister."

Like best friends armed with our inside jokes and our increasing roster of shared experiences, it begins to feel like whatever comes, we'll face it together. Justin clears out a drawer for me to keep my stuff in at his place. He talks about getting me my own keys so I can come and go as I please. My artist residency in Vancouver runs out, and I look for new work in a city I don't fit into because I'm in a relationship that feels like it's getting better. Justin wants me to take more trips with him. There's no part of my budget that can accommodate more time without wages, so I dig further into personal debt. I want the companionship, and I want to feel like even if I'm broke, at least I'm living a life less ordinary. It's the kind of logic that's easy to fall into when you've been raised without a sense of permanence to anything and when you've never pictured owning assets or having retirement savings. The door's still open for intimacy outside of our intimacy, and Justin knows that Evie and I have an ongoing play dynamic, but he also knows that I haven't seen Evie in half a year. I know that Justin likes me, but I also know that he likes the chase—and I know that my own capacity for romantic melodrama is spent. Our bond feels positive but tenuous.

I'm drumming up jobs so I can stop maxing out debt products, when Justin swings by one of my work meetings and hits on my colleague Logan.

Justin's comfortable with his own orientation, but he's never developed a comfortable way of expressing it. It's a repeating issue I've had some patience for because I understand where it comes from. Between the social conditioning he's had, the fact that he has an ex-wife, and the fact that most of us queers are assumed straight until we find a way to out ourselves, Justin uses flirtation as his self-outing mechanism.

It's one of the subtle ways that structural erasure can negatively impact queer behaviour. It leaves us queer people in a position to use bad tactics to solve problems that aren't of our making. I've met plenty of queer men who have convinced themselves they're incapable of sexual harassment, and any complaints about their conduct are a misunderstanding of the ways they're being self-expressive and charming.

There is a line between charm and harm. That line has come and gone when Justin offers Logan a taste of his drink by sliding his finger between Logan's lips.

Justin's need to be seen costs me the jobs I've been drumming up; it's too uncomfortable for Logan and me to work together after the way Justin's behaved. He costs me months of project planning and future cash money and embarrasses the shit out of me. He does not clock the impact of his actions on my finances because he makes over $100K annually and sees the poverty wages I scrap for in the arts as inconsequential. Mostly, he doesn't register that I need income at all. For Justin, dating is about having companions in adventure. Beyond condoms and lube, there's no room for life practicalities in his RV.

I set a new boundary with Justin about his sex life and my work contacts: no hitting on my colleagues.

He responds to my boundary by dumping me over email.

He packs up the contents of my drawer in a reusable bag from a high-end Kitsilano grocery store and drops off my stuff beside the entrance to Now and Always.

"This is how queer guys behave, so if you think you're a boy … I don't know what you were expecting," his email reads.

For months after our breakup, I walk around by myself with a cigarette between my fingers and a joint tucked behind my ear, alternating from sucking on one to the other.

Cherry blossoms fall from the trees and blanket the streets in pink poetry while I'm feeling fucked up by Justin's swipe at my gender. I'm fucked up by the fact that when trans people assert our boundaries in relationships, cis people gaslight us about our gender identities—even though personal boundaries and gender expression have nothing to do with one another.

During my months of processing, TERFs show up to the city's Dyke March with anti-trans slurs written on big rocks, bringing a whole new meaning to the idea of getting stoned in Vancouver.

I think about how, in the short time I've been calling myself non-binary, the information has been treated as meaningless or actively used against me—and all by people who would describe themselves as left-leaning fans of the rainbow flag. The call's coming from inside the house. It's more than unsettling.

If being non-binary is stepping outside of the social construct of gender, then coming out about being non-binary is a step toward learning how instinctively people will uphold the construct of gender, past the limits of kindness, rationality, or integrity.

These experiences—the social media stalking, the anti-trans actions in queer spaces, the lover I made love to passionately who then jabbed at where I'm most vulnerable—all roll around the inside of my head when I'm awake and asleep. I have recurrent nightmares about not being able to get what I need. In them, I flip open the first cellphone I ever had and dial 9-1-1 on the keypad, but the wrong numbers keep showing up on the screen: 5-3-4, 2-6-9, 3-2-2. I wake up sticky with sweat, stare at the ceiling, and decide I have to get my shit together.

I did not survive my childhood to be broken by other people's self-serving perspectives, their emotional abuse, or their genuine lack of imagination. I did not come out to feel bad about who I am. I've been hit before, many times. I know how to get knocked down. I know how to get back up.

I quit sex for the first time in my adult life. In the grand scheme of things, it's not a very long pause, but it's enough time for me to rewire my brain to stop treating sex like a safety blanket.

I get a new job in the arts based in a city other than Vancouver or Toronto. Physically, I'm more or less still based out of Vancity and work remotely on new artistic projects in different provinces. My life revolves around my MacBook, finding cheap flights, and doing laundry whenever I'm near someone with a washing machine. I'm on the road. I've gone on three dates with Kyle, and we're setting up a fourth for when I'm back in BC.

I want you to bring your harness, Kyle texts me.

The fun thing about being on the road when you've just starting dating someone is that it slows down the pace of the relationship without diminishing the excitement. Kyle and I share daily text updates, send each other what we're listening to on Spotify, and have three-hour phone calls about living with anxiety and what it's like to go off antidepressants while he curls up on his daybed in Vancouver and I kick a pebble around a parking lot in Calgary.

The closer it gets to me being back in BC, the more pent-up and graphic our text chats get. I like it. I've always liked sexting, and because of the weeks of chats, sexting with Kyle doesn't feel like sexting with a stranger.

Kyle wants me to bring the strap-on harness I'm using for sex these days, which he's heard me lovingly describe but has never seen. It's shiny black patent leather on the outside, lined with black suede that rests against the skin at my hips, and it's made for the Japanese market, so unlike many mass-market sex aids, it fits my small five-foot frame. It's tight and ornate. When I wear it with my imitation horsehair butt plug in my ass at the same time, I feel like a soft butch dreamboat crossed with a My Little Pony.

Kyle doesn't need to ask me to bring my harness.

I've had my harness and fuck cock in my backpack every time I've shown up at your place, I text Kyle.

Really!

It's my body. I bring my body when I see you.

Makes sense to me. I've been missing out on dick unnecessarily!

Seriously.

Kyle leans into his greedy bottom vibes hard, and I can roll with it even though it makes me feel like I'm aging out of relating to twentysomethings. I can tell that this persona he slips into around intimacy is the surface layer of some larger truth, though I can't put my finger on what the truth is. He's at a place in life where it's helpful for him to distill his personality into a phrase, like a brand rather than a person, and that phrase happens to be "cock-hungry slut." He reminds me of myself in my adolescence, with my push-up bras and low-rise jeans. At the same time, he doesn't fetishize my gender or want it to have a particular shape or form.

Whether I show up in a tit-hugging crop top or with my chest bound, he has the same nonchalance about it. My gender expression is a non-topic between us. Whatever I look like when I show up, he hugs me, cracks open a craft beer, and starts telling me what's exasperated him during his workday of designing concrete foundations.

Unlike Kyle, his squad is weird about having a trans person in the mix.

I have a deep conversation with one of Kyle's toxic ex-girlfriends about my pronouns, and the next time I run into her, she makes sure to loudly misgender me.

The self-described mama bear of the squad invites me to all group excursions and BBQs but also makes sure to tell Kyle, in front of me, about all the gorgeous outdoorsy cis women she wants to set him up with.

On a coffee catch-up with a friend, Kyle mentions that the new person he's dating is non-binary, and his friend responds, "I don't agree with hormone blockers for kids."

"Well, my partner isn't a child, so we're covered there," Kyle answers.

It's a real-life crappy dream for me that a partner who is so cool comes with such gross baggage. It's a waking nightmare for Kyle, realizing what kind of people his friends are.

We find capacity to be horny in spite of these microaggressions.

I get back to Vancouver and show up at Kyle's door in Yaletown with my backpack full of my hard-on.

I fumble to get my shoes off in the doorway, while he's already lifted up my oversized T-shirt to suck on my tits.

I take his hand and lead him to his bedroom, bend him over his bed, and slide the hem of his jersey dress up over the juicy ass that I know so well from his GIFs.

"It's all yours, Sly," he says.

He slides his face and upper body onto the bed like a snake so he can use both hands to spread his ass cheeks wide open. His sphincter's already contracting and opening.

I roll him onto his back on his bed so he can watch. I lose my clothes efficiently, rather than in a strip tease, while Kyle rubs his erection through the thong he's wearing. His cock is so swollen it's pushing through the holes in the lace, imprinting roses and flower petals all over the underside of his dick.

I turn away from him and slip on my black-patent-leather harness, with my hard fuck cock slipped through the O-ring.

"Give me a drumroll, lover."

Kyle drums out anticipation on the thick thighs he's cultivated with his personal trainer. I spin around, covering up my nerves with a show.

"Bam!"

"You look beautiful! Get over here!" he exclaims.

"You like all of me?"

"I like all of you. I want to suck on your cock. Can I suck on your cock?"

"Yes, please."

His pouty lips touch the tip of the head of my cock, then slowly open, and his tongue flicks the indentation at the tip of my cock where a urethra should be.

"Holy shit, Kyle, that's good."

He opens his lips more. He slides his lips toward me and wraps his whole mouth around the head of my cock. He looks up at me, swirls his tongue around the head of my dick, and closes his eyes as he slowly slides more of my cock into his mouth.

"Oh shit, holy shit."

I can't explain how I can physically feel Kyle deep throating my cock, but I can.

His mouth releases its vacuum seal from my cock, and we lock eyes. His eyes are wide. I feel so close to him. Strangers jerk off to him daily, and I've lost track of the number of people I've had sex with. We both, off and on, have tried to trade anonymous access to our naked selves for the sense that our gender expressions are sexy. We're both still genuinely surprised by moments of real intimacy. We stay in this moment, the smell of our bodies hanging heavy in the air between us, holding very still as we take each other in.

"Could you try calling me 'she'?"

"Absolutely," I answer.

I straddle Kyle, kiss her, lie her down on her bed, and lift her dress up to her neck. I go to town on her nipples, and she moans, twitches, feels every bit of it. Her nipples don't numb to the sensation, and I love it. I could lick her nipples forever. My cock's pressing into her stomach, and I can feel her lace-clad cock pressing into my thigh.

"Do you want to be inside me?" I ask her.

"Yes, I want to!"

I climb off her and lie back on her bed while she crawls to her nightstand. She slides on a condom and waddles back on her knees to my outstretched legs.

I spit on my hands and rub one palmful of spit into my labia, another onto my dick.

Kyle slips her cock into my cunt slowly, and I grasp my cock tight.

I've felt a lot of things slide into my cunt, and nothing's ever felt as good sliding into me as when I can feel my own cock simultaneously.

She slides her cock in and out of me, over and over, while I run my palm, curled around my cock, up and down in time with her movements.

I can feel all of it, everywhere.

"I can feel this everywhere, and it feels so fucking good, Kyle."

"I love watching you stroke yourself while I fuck you!"

"I love it too."

I love looking at Kyle's dilated pupils in the dim light of her bedroom and the beads of sweat where her beautiful face meets her hair.

"Do you want to come with me inside you?" I ask her.

She answers by sliding herself out of me, crawling toward the pillows at the head of her bed, and raising her ass into the air.

I've never seen a sphincter look so ready or inviting.

I lube my cock.

I lube her asshole, slowly.

I stand on my knees.

With a lot of calm and a lot of check-ins with Kyle about what feels good, we take our time sliding my cock inside her.

As I gently fuck her, sweat builds at my hairline from the care I take to move with slow control. I can feel her ass contracting around me, I can feel my swollen clit, I can feel how wet my cunt is, I can see her fingertips digging into her own ass cheeks as she spreads her ass open wider. She smiles at me.

"Deeper," she mouths.

I go deeper, slowly, hit her prostate, and feel her shudder around me. Her eyes widen, and her face flushes.

"That's the spot?"

She nods, eyes wide, and I dedicate myself to watching her come buckets.

I curl my whole body around her upturned ass.

Every inch of me that's touching every inch of her holds a world of importance, no matter the parts of our bodies or whether or not they are body parts we were born with. Our intimacy teaches us how to understand each other and how to see ourselves.

I press my face against her spine, kiss her skin, and think of us as line drawings scrawled hastily on the wall of a dive bar bathroom. Somewhere, there's a drawing of Kyle, her big eyes, her joyful smile, in a pink sundress holding a VR headset. Somewhere there's a drawing of me with big tits and a dick poking out of the top of my jeans. Written in Sharpie up the length of the vein at the base of my shaft are the words "I love you."

Kyle comes all over her stomach, all over her pillows, and all over the bed underneath us. We stay still, just breathing.

As she falls asleep in her bed next to me, I think about the question of transition, about what I am, and about who Kyle might be.

For so many of the trans and non-binary people I know, there's a trajectory. Hormone replacement therapy, followed by approvals for surgery or surgeries, followed by surgeries and recoveries.

There's also investing in a whole new wardrobe and spending the time, money, and emotional labour to change gender markers on IDs.

There's coming out to friends, family, and colleagues.

It's harder than puberty and a difficult process physically, emotionally, and financially—one the health care system, employers, and governments need to make easier and need to take more seriously. I have deep respect for the toll it takes on people in my community. I have deep respect for the people in my community who know they need to go through that process because it's what's right for them. I also feel deep frustration that, in the society we live in, gender is endlessly enforced as a binary, because it means conversations about transition and gender diversity are forced to form themselves around a fallacious duality.

I've heard cis people describe non-binary identity as being halfway between being a man and a woman, or being a bit of both. I've fallen into the habit of describing myself in those terms too, at different points, as I grasp for anything that's recognizable, articulable, or validated by cisgender society. But being non-binary isn't about being a bit of both, because there isn't a both in the first place.

There are variations in body anatomy, and then there are socially constructed concepts of manhood and womanhood that society attaches to these anatomical attributes, as if everyone who is tall has to be a basketball player and every person with perfect pitch has to sing.

The fact that we have the right to understand ourselves on our own terms and to transition from M to F, or from F to M, is still a battle in some places and still a work in progress in others. I'm grateful for those battles and humbled by that work. At the same time, for me, it's not F to M, it's F to something else entirely. F to X, in which M is part of the equation but not the answer.

As trans and non-binary people, even though we look at, subvert, and step outside of the gender constructs we were assigned at birth, we're still using the clumsy language of binary gender to try to convey who we are because we don't have a better language at our disposal. I've had other trans and non-binary people talk to me about feeling like aliens, because how can our minds work the way they do if we're really from this world?

One day we might have a better language at our disposal that can't be leveraged against us. Until then, I use words like "trans," "they," and "them," despite the complications they come with in cisgender society, because they're words that assert the truth: regardless of whether or not I'm from this world, I am definitely real.

Kyle lies on her bed beside me. She talks in her sleep, and I hear her side of her dream conversations. She sounds happy. I listen to her and fall asleep, knowing that words fall short in describing identity now, and maybe they always will.

That doesn't mean that we exist in agony, though. It just means that words are so much smaller than our souls.

FLUFFER

"Can I shout a string of obscenities at you?"

It's been about six months since I was in Toronto last and longer than that since I've seen Evie. We decide to meet at a bar called Gorgeous Garbage in Toronto's west side, not too far from the house owned by Evie's investment banker boyfriend. GG is a cool small-capacity cocktail bar at the back of a storefront sushi counter—the kind of place you'd blink and miss if you didn't know it was there. It's part of the growing trend in bars on the west side that are either rich kid hobby businesses or about to go belly up because they aren't getting enough foot traffic to make a profit. They're the best bars to catch up with a lover at because no one ever asks you to leave, not even if you've been nursing the ice water in your glass for hours. Evie and I have a lot to catch up on.

Evie never seems to age, change her vibe, or try out a new haircut. Like one of the characters on *The Simpsons*, she always looks the same, regardless of how much time has gone by or what world events have happened. Her existence weaves in and out of the world the rest of us live in like a needle pushing through and pulling out of fabric. Her day-to-day is tied to her website advertising her services, her Craigslist ad, and booking emails from her clients, who are mostly very rich cisgender men. Outside of travel, work, and recovering from the physical and emotional impact of her labour, Evie goes to the gym, trains in mixed martial arts, hangs out at her boyfriend's, and sees play partners like me. It's a way of living where there's a fair amount of freedom but also isolation and precarity. She handles the stress of her career through unrestrained online shopping, being friends with other cis women in her field, and snorting cocaine.

As my career as an artist takes form, I begin to feel what that kind of freedom, isolation, and precarity is like while I mount shows, get grants, and live on and off planes. I have no more nine-to-five, but I'm constantly looking for gigs, so it never feels like I'm not working. I go to daytime yoga classes in Vancouver's Gastown with wealthy divorcees and underemployed TV actors. I find it difficult to be friends with people who aren't in my industry even though I miss having a life outside of work. I operate with a short fuse, though having compassion and insight is what I'm supposed to do professionally. The people I work with discuss how all gender is a performance but treat my gender identity as both a fabrication and a social justice rebranding opportunity. I handle the stress of my career by treating coffee catch-ups like therapy, rewatching TV shows I've already seen a hundred times, and fantasizing about living alone in the middle of nowhere.

I'm always nervous when I'm about to see Evie even though we've been lovers so casually and consistently that it feels like we might keep playing together forever. It's a summer evening in Toronto. The late evening sun pours in around her as she whips open the velvet curtain hanging over the bar's doorway. She spots me, and I wave like a happy kid about to go on a class trip to somewhere exciting.

"I thought I'd be theatrical about it since you're an artist now." Evie smiles.

We make out at the bar. Kissing is the least intimate thing we do. I always laugh on the inside at how unsexy our kissing is. We kiss when we meet in public as the socially acceptable substitute for her gagging and torturing me, which is where our intimacy thrives.

"I'm the same person, only now without three-hundred-dollar underwear. Unless I can write it into a costume budget."

"Your hair's gone grey."

"I've actually been grey for a while. I've just stopped dyeing it."

"What else has changed?"

I've been working through the fact that I'm not cisgender for a long time, but I've never brought it up with Evie. Keeping the ongoing revelation to myself meant that our interactions were focused on our play. It kept our lives separated, and it meant that I didn't have to gamble on my gender reveal changing our dom/sub dynamic.

It's easier to reveal myself onstage than it is to say something vulnerable to the real people who know me. One-on-one, the risk feels greater. But tonight, I've decided to come out to my long-time lover, and she's just handed me a segue.

"I only use they and them pronouns now. I've realized I'm trans and non-binary."

"That's great, Sly! I'm so happy for you."

I notice how much my heart is pinballing around my chest. I drink a lot of the drink that's in front of me.

"Thank you. It's good. It's a journey, but it's good."

"That's a big deal, and I'm proud of you."

I make puppy sounds and nuzzle at her collarbone with my nose while she looks at the drink menu.

I'd been planning on easing into updating Evie on my pronouns and gender, so the efficiency of our exchange is jarring. A seismic shift feels like it should take more than a few words to convey.

I feel vulnerable, frail, and strangely empty. I'm glad she knows what the terminology means and that I don't have to justify or explain. At the same time, there's a hollowness that I can't rationalize—so I act happy and figure the emptiness I feel will go away.

"I think I have a binder at my apartment that's about your size. I'll have you try it on," Evie offers.

"Oh. Okay."

"And there's a trans sex worker I follow on FetLife. When they had top surgery, they decided to forgo having nipples. I'll have to show you. They're so unique."

"That sounds … great."

The bar's lone staff member comes over to us.

"Do you ladies need anything?"

"I'm going to have a glass of red wine, but we aren't ladies. It's important that you not make assumptions. My date is non-binary," Evie answers.

Her rapid-fire assumptions and allyship give me whiplash. What's happening, now?

Have I asked for a chest binder? Am I affirmed by my date telling off a service worker? Is it Evie's place to tell people who I am? Most confusing of all: would I be a more compelling trans person without my nipples?

"It's on me, Sly. We're celebrating you."

I look at the bartender and see a tired guy working a slow shift where he's not going to make much on tips. I feel sorry for him and annoyed at Evie in a way I don't know how to process.

My earlobes are hot. It's as if Evie's more interested in her performance of graciousness than she is in the way her actions are really impacting the people around her.

"I'll have the most expensive drink you make," I tell the bartender.

I decide to shift the spotlight off me. I won't be able to figure out how I feel about how this conversation has gone until the bright light is out of my eyes.

I ask Evie to tell me anything she wants about what's new for her. The bartender serves her a glass of red and starts working on my top-shelf drink, and Evie goes into a long-form update.

She's officially divorced. Her ex-husband still sends her dick pics, and the two of them still text to talk about his depression and to jerk off to each other.

Her best friend, Lucy, is in town and staying in one of the extra bedrooms at Evie's boyfriend's place. Lucy's a sex worker, and she and Evie spend their daytimes alone together in the big, multimillion-dollar home that investment banking can buy. They love every giddy, luxurious moment of it, like teens in a *Clueless* meets *Spring Breakers* crossover. Lucy says she can feel the wealth in the walls. She and Evie rub their breasts against the marble in the bathroom while speaking spells made up by Lucy so the wealth will magically rub off on both of them. They're in proximity to financial security, but for now at least, it still isn't theirs.

Michael, the investment banker boyfriend, is loving having two women running around his house, rubbing their breasts on his things.

Evie's worried about having lost some of her regular clients over the last year and what that means for her bottom line. She's still got enough cash flow coming in—for now. She's going to keep the lease on her condo but test drive moving into Michael's place. If she were able to stop paying both rent on her condo and the mortgage on her dungeon, it would take some pressure off. Michael's been trying to get her to move in and trying to leverage his wealth to lock down their relationship for as long as they've been sleeping together.

Evie's going to buy a beagle once Lucy leaves so she doesn't have to spend her days in her boyfriend's big house all alone.

"Moving in with Michael means that he can walk the dog or pay someone to walk the dog when I'm away for work."

I don't know how to tell her that I'm worried about the choices she's making. Our play dynamic has never involved giving each other life advice.

At the same time, the increasing financial pressures of living in Canada's major cities means that hardly anyone that I know is in a position to make decisions about who they live with without being swayed by the money side of it. Rents across the country are going through the roof. So I say things about her plan that are bland and supportive.

"Mm-hmm! Dogs are great."

She pulls out her phone and shows me pictures from the Grand Canyon hike she recently went on with one of her American clients. It's a unique feeling, looking at a face I know very well next to the face of a rich guy who pays her. She's never shown me any of her clients before. I'm not sure why she's inviting me into more of her existence now. Maybe my openness has elicited hers. Both Evie and her client are smiling at the camera, like a May–December romance selfie with a backdrop of one of the world's greatest wonders.

"I'm going to be in town while you're here, so we can have a few dates, if you want to. I've already told Michael I'm going to be seeing you," Evie says.

The first date we plan as we dive back into kink with each other is at Evie's condo. She orders bougie delivery pizza, and we sit at her kitchen island and make small talk as best we can. We've done the catch-up thing already at Gorgeous Garbage. We're both ready to be raw with each other.

I've been to Evie's dungeon many times, but it's the first time I've seen her condo. I look around her home, knowing it probably won't be her home much longer. It feels like I'm always arriving places on the eve of their demise—in Vancouver once it's lost its grit and open-mindedness, in Toronto as it's losing its creativity, and at James's Shibari Salon as it fades into a distant memory, the yearbook inscriptions in the doorway painted over and forgotten.

I wonder if I'll ever arrive somewhere on the cusp of its invention so that, at least for a while, I'll have somewhere to stay.

Evie's home, unlike her dungeon, is nearly devoid of personality and pushes the boundaries of what could be described as minimalism. The kitchen is barely used and completely spotless. She struggles to locate where the dish soap is stowed. The living room has a futon mattress sitting directly on the floor, facing a huge flat-screen TV that also sits on the floor, and there's a sad, lone houseplant in the corner. Her bedroom is composed of an old wooden dresser that looks like it was picked up at a garage sale, a tall mirror leaned against the wall and adorned with Christmas lights, and a mattress sitting directly on the floor, just like the futon in the living room. The third room of her condo is a library, with a full wall of books facing a small teak desk, and this is the room that strikes me as strangest of all because Evie never talks about reading. The lone piece of art in the condo is a small framed drawing of a Rottweiler, the dog's mouth hanging open, with octopus tentacles reaching out from somewhere deep inside the dog's throat. I stare at the tentacle suckers clinging to the Rottweiler's teeth, reaching toward the unknown.

If I didn't know Evie, I'd feel like I was standing in the home of a serial killer. Because I do know her, I feel like I'm standing in the home of someone who's been on the run from a complicated childhood for a long time and who hasn't really stopped running.

"Do you identify with the Rottweiler or the octopus?"

"I identify with the deep-throating," she answers.

"Do you remember the first time we played, when you made me your dog?"

"I remember."

She asks me if I've had enough pizza, then immediately takes the box out to stuff it down the garbage chute. Her home is barren and precise. Even a pizza box out of place would bring chaos to the order. Like the first time we played, Evie always moves with purpose.

When she comes back, she asks if she can wash me. I take off my clothes. My cunt is already anticipating our play; I can feel it like it's been bolded and underlined. I can smell it. I stand in her bathtub. Evie washes me, towels me, picks me up, and stands me on the bathroom tiles in front of her.

"Spread the towel out on the futon and then lie down on it," she instructs me.

I do so. My subspace brain is already kicking in.

I've played with Evie for years, so my body anticipates the joy that's in store even though she and I never prenegotiate the details of our scenes. She doesn't have to say or do much to turn me on. As I lie naked on the damp towel on her futon, I might as well be crawling around a kennel cage. In my peripheral vision, I can see her stripping naked, pulling on a crop top, and moving around her barely used kitchen, looking for something.

She comes back to the living room with the shirt on, but nothing below the waist, like Porky Pig. She's holding a tall takeout soup container. She reaches down to my feet, holds both my ankles in one hand, and lifts my feet up so my knees are folded into my torso. She instructs me to hold my legs there. She runs her fingers over my ass and inner thighs, just outside the periphery of my unruly pubic hair. She stands on the futon with her feet facing my ass cheeks and looks down at me.

It is always in play that Evie and I are at our most connected. The weirdness I felt at the bar about her overbearing allyship melts away.

I have no idea what she's got in mind for our scene, but when it comes to kink, I trust her completely.

She places the soup container between my calves, with the mouth of the container facing up at her. She tells me to hold it there, steady. She slides her body over my legs and the container so she's straddling both.

"Now, you're my toilet," Evie says.

She pisses into the container as I hold it tightly between my legs. I moan, groan, and feel every moment of it.

I hear the piss, smell it, and feel the weight of the container increasing between my calves.

I feel the warmth above me, and I watch her piss collecting through the foggy, translucent plastic.

Everything in my body reacts to being her toilet. I'm like a kid at Christmas.

I can't move without spilling piss everywhere, so I stay as still as I can. I try to be as competent in my physical task as I can be. In this stillness, I let the pleasure of being made useful spill through me, everywhere. I feel delight, from my bones through to my nail beds.

For me, there's a difference between being useful and being used. In kink, I like the feeling of being useful because it releases me from the burden of wondering what my life means.

I like bottoming that makes me feel like I'm being good just by being there. I like feeling like I don't need to do very much at all to be appreciated. It's not unconditional love, but it mimics it, because in kink I like to feel unconditionally treasured.

The difference between the bottoming I do and submitting to being used might be hard to see, but it's there.

I'm turned on and in awe of Evie's body as her piss pours and trickles into the container. I think about the first time I saw her play at Feast and how unscripted and instinctive all her ideas seemed then, and still now. Time and space fold. I can't believe that the same woman I watched beating an ass blue in a dungeon now sees me as worthy of being her toilet.

"I love you, Evie."

"I love you too, Sly," she says, piss still trickling.

She takes the container from between my legs and walks out of my line of vision.

I continue to lie on the futon, my legs still holding their toilet position. I won't move any part of me until Evie tells me to. I don't want to move until she tells me to. I can still feel every moment of being a toilet and being in love reverberating through me. I feel seen. I feel like the rest of my life is an act, where I pretend to be a person who's content to be part of the normal world, when in reality, I'm choking on it. I feel like I'm finally the real me.

Evie comes back into view, still Porky Pigging it, but now in a strap-on harness with a dildo locked into the O-ring. She kneels on the futon, facing my ass, her dildo grazing my labia between my upturned legs.

"Do you know how to deep throat, toilet?" she asks me.

"I don't. I'm terrible at it. When I give head, I use both hands on the shaft and basically just suck the tip. Or I'll just choke."

"I'll have to train you."

Evie slides her dildo into my cunt. My cunt is swollen and wet from our piss play. She braces herself on my upturned calves and fucks me hard and fast—like she's fucking me to survive, fucking me to work something out.

"Can I rub my clit?"

"Yes," she answers.

I lick my fingers and rub my clit while she fucks me faster and more severely, but still controlled. She never moves with abandon; she hammers into my cunt with purpose.

Her dildo is covered in my fluids; they splash onto her stomach, her harness, and the hemline of her shirt.

I don't know when or if she's ever going to stop fucking me.

I don't think I care.

Her dildo is hard, stiff, and unforgiving inside me. My brain's slipping into subspace again, and I see myself from outside myself. I'm made of white porcelain, like a bathroom fixture crossed with something out of the mind of David Lynch. Evie kneels at the base of the porcelain fixture, fucking my glazed, painted porcelain vulva with her merciless dildo. Octopuses crawl out of her mouth and squelch as they tumble off the futon and hit the floor of the living room, while she gasps for air.

I ejaculate all over her.

Slowly, I come back to a more typical way of seeing reality. Evie pulls her dildo out of me, scoops me up in her arms, and carries me back to her bathroom.

The container of her piss sits on the edge of the bathtub. She lowers me gently into the tub, takes off her harness, and leaves the dildo covered in my come on the ledge of the bathroom sink, standing upright like a tower. She unties her messy hair, turns the bathtub faucet on, makes the water warm, and sits down in the tub across from me. Warm water pours out of the tap and pools around my bum, heels, and toes.

Evie picks up the container of her piss and carefully pours some of her pee over the back of my head, down my neck and over my shoulders. A queer kink baptism. She gently pours the rest of her piss into her own wild wheat-coloured hair.

I am deep in subspace and completely non-verbal. Even if I had something to say, I couldn't speak if I tried. The things I'm feeling don't exist in words. The thoughts and images I'm experiencing are random and complex, coherent and incomprehensible, like my psyche is pinballing around the galaxy. I feel awake, alive, tranquil, receptive, like I'm living what is meant to be my real life rather than moving through a bland facsimile.

Evie tells me to put the stopper into the drain. I do it. The tub begins to fill up with warm water. She shampoos my head, neck, and shoulders, then shampoos and rinses her own long hair, filling the tub with soap suds.

We sit together in the bath, silently listening to the drum of the tub filling with water.

"Sly, if it's all right with you, I'm going to sit here and cry for three minutes."

I nod and watch Evie cry. She's never cried in front of me before. She doesn't wail, sob, or scream. She doesn't try to suppress her tears. She cries, quietly but consistently, for about three minutes. When she stops crying, she asks if I'd like to sleep over. I don't ask why she was crying, and she doesn't offer an explanation.

The next morning, Evie and I wake up next to each other on the mattress she keeps on the floor of her bedroom. She always comes to wide awake, suddenly; I come to consciousness slowly, while she gets up and begins bounding around her day.

She brings out the chest binder she mentioned to me at GGs. I'm verbal again but still spacey, in a receptive and accepting state, so I'm not annoyed by the binder offer now the way I was at the bar. I try it on, and it's too big, so Evie keeps it. She makes a mini French press of coffee. We make plans for another date, this time at Fountain, and Evie asks if I'd mind if Lucy and her date tag along with us.

"Yes to absolutely everything, Evie."

She kisses me goodbye in the doorway. I stop at a hipster coffee shop in a neighbourhood filled with families. A kid in line near me asks their mom if I'm a boy or a girl, and the mom chastises her kid. I'm not even sure if I'm a person at all. I tell the kid that I might be a bit of all the atoms in existence.

"I don't know what that means!" the kid barks at me.

It feels like a lifetime ago that I was annoyed at Evie, even though we were just at GG. I came out to her about being non-binary, and we're still lovers and play partners. We still bend space, time, and the fabric of the universe with each other. She still cares for me, and she's still the most magnificent, creative, and boundless dominant I've ever known.

The euphoria I feel from being Evie's toilet just keeps going and going, like the Energizer Bunny.

A week later, I'm at Fountain, sitting on a bar stool with my back to the stripper pole, waiting for Evie, Lucy, and Lucy's date to arrive.

It's the second date Evie and I will have during my work trip to Toronto this time around, and it feels significant. We don't usually see each other this much. She's usually busier with clients, and maybe that's all there is to us seeing more of each other. Or maybe our bond is deepening.

Naked strangers walk by me. I take in the faint smell of latex and chlorine. I used to come here often. While the venue's the same, most of the staff have turned over. No one recognizes me. A group of tentative twentysomethings comes into the club together, pushing each other to take penguin steps into the space. What's old is new, and what's new is old. Cities—and strongholds of subcultures, like Fountain—hold so many experiences but so little memory. We who search for ourselves and for our place in the world come and go from these settings, while the setting itself barely notices.

Evie comes in with a bag of toys in hand, along with a high femme who I assume is Lucy and Lucy's date.

Lucy's got a round face, dark caramel eyes, and long, silky black-brown hair. She has deeply pockmarked cheeks, and her scars accentuate and draw attention to how beautiful she is. She's slender and strong without being ripped, like someone who knows the cash value return on doing Pilates every morning. She carries herself like she knows she's sexy, which makes her even sexier. She's wearing red patent-leather heels and a wet-look fire-engine-red PVC minidress, with cleavage for days. She finds a way to swing her long hair around her with almost every move she makes, like someone who has mastered the art of hairography. Whereas Evie commands attention without trying, Lucy's presence commands attention in a way that says, "Yes, I'm trying to get you to look at me—but don't pretend you don't love it." She moves like a hustler—not like a person who is presently hustling, but like a person whose sense of self and ability to acquire and accumulate things have become the same thing. It's a powerful vibe, a little terrifying and exciting.

Evie detaches from the squad she's arrived with to say hello.

"That's Lucy in the red?"

"That's Lucy."

"She's incredible."

"She is! You can feel it?" Evie asks, surprised.

"Oh yeah. From across the room. Immediately."

Evie squeals with delight.

"Come meet Lucy."

It's a funny moment because it feels so easy, but this is more of Evie's social circle than I've encountered in our years of playing together.

Lucy's date is smaller, slimmer, and quiet. They have big dark eyes and dark peach fuzz on their upper lip. The hair on their head is short, but it's gotten messy as it's grown out. It adds to the air of ambivalence that hangs around them. They're definitely present of their own will—they don't look like they're being coerced. They do, however, look like someone who needs a very big, very long hug. They're an adult, but beyond that, their age is hard to pinpoint beyond a broad range—anywhere from nineteen to thirty-three. A lot of us trans and masc-of-centre folks are Peter Pans, a group of perpetually lost boys who never age. I don't need to wait to hear that Lucy's date is trans, because I can feel it. Like me, Lucy's date was assigned a female identity at birth. They take off their street clothes to reveal the fetish gear they're wearing underneath. They're wearing a men's leather chest harness that carves a black horizonal line across their chest; their tiny breasts and pointy nipples poke out underneath.

I shake hands with Lucy as Evie introduces us.

I turn to Lucy's date.

"This is my fluffer," Lucy says.

I shake the date's hand. Their handshake is limp, like their heart isn't in in. Their eyes barely meet mine. It's no one's job to want to meet me, but the combination of lack of eye contact, the passivity in their hands, and the label—fluffer—weirds me out.

I've met a lot of bottoms, subs, baby girls, rope sluts, and littles in kink, and in different ways, at different points, most of these labels have applied to me. Fetish is a big tent with a variety of options for releasing tension, and that's one of the things I like about it—it expands my sense of the world, my understanding of self-authorship, consent, catharsis, and individuality. Kink makes me a less judgmental person. But the fact that kink is a big tent doesn't mean that there aren't also problematic dynamics, abusers, and harmful acts within it that compound existing trauma or create new trauma.

The term "fluffer" is out of pornography rather than specifically out of kink. On a porn set, a fluffer is a person who is employed off-camera to get a performer's penis hard or to keep a performer's penis erect in between takes. The person being serviced by a fluffer is usually a cis man, and the fluffer is usually a cis woman—at least as far as mainstream straight porn goes.

If Lucy and the fluffer are engaged in some long-form, no-break role play that started before they got to the club, no one's told me. If Lucy's hired this person and is paying them, that's cool—except my instincts are telling me that isn't the case. I've agreed to hang out with Evie and her best friend tonight, who are both cisgender femmes, and now I'm meeting another trans person, like me—and the other trans person is being given a function, but no name.

None of this necessarily adds up to the fact that something harmful is happening, but the facts still unsettle me. I want trans people to have names.

For the second time on this trip to Toronto, I wonder about who I am to Evie, now that I'm a trans person she plays with as opposed to who she used to understand me to be.

I don't like feeling so unsure around Evie when I've always trusted her. Her presence has always made me nervous but has never felt like a threat. The four of us move deeper into Fountain, to the room with a stage, where like before, Sybian rides are taking place. I make conversation with Lucy in hopes that knowing her better will put me at ease.

We chat about Vancity, where I'm still based. Lucy loves coming to Vancouver for work and does so often. She loves coming into town for the Vancouver International Film Festival and crashing industry parties so she can meet semifamous film folk and turn them into her clients. She tells me about chatting up a Canadian TV actor all night, telling him he could pay her for sex, and then, as they headed to his place, steps away from his door, he turned to her and said she must be kidding about him paying because he wasn't the kind of guy who needed to pay for it.

"It was such a waste of my night, because every guy is the kind of guy who needs to pay for it," Lucy tells me. "If you want a healthy relationship with your own sex life, don't do sex work. Even if I'm attracted to someone, I still think about what I can get out of them by having sex with them. The thought's always there."

While Lucy and I chat, on the other side of the room, Evie's getting cozier with the fluffer. She's ruffling the fluffer's hair. It's making me even more uneasy. Evie and I have zero exclusivity, but at the same time, we've never gone on a date together and failed to be the centre of each other's attention. I'm cool with cucks—I've met joyful, empowered cucks who truly, deeply dig watching their partner fuck someone else instead of them—but watching my date get down with someone else on our date isn't my thing. I suggest to Lucy that we join the two of them.

"I was bitching to Sly about a time in Vancouver when I wasted my night trying to drum up business," Lucy tells Evie.

"Guys from Vancouver waste everybody's time. They dangle the promise of being what you want, like a carrot on a stick, so they can fuck you from behind and crush you with their insecurities," I say.

Lucy laughs.

"You'd do well as a sex worker in Vancouver, Sly," Evie says. "You're so small, men with small cocks would love fucking you."

Evie's never talked to me this way before.

As she sits closer to Lucy's fluffer, I can't tell what is happening.

Is Evie just being matter of fact, or flippant? Is she showing off in front of the fluffer and her best friend? Is she trying to put me down because I made a crack about cis men, and she feels called out by it because her primary partner is one? Has she collated data on BC dick dimensions?

Has our status with each other changed?

I have no hang-ups about sex work. I know many trans folk who do sex work—because they've been barred from or discriminated against in typical work environments, for the benefit and flexibility of setting their own working hours and conditions, in order to fund the costs of medical transition, as a matter of simple preference and choice, and for countless other individual reasons. Sex work is manual labour, and sex work is work, full stop. It should be legalized, and it shouldn't be stigmatized. Sex work should be respected and given the same labour law protections as any other industry.

At the same time, I'm building a career as an artist, and Evie knows this.

While I work on being part of the arts industry, I'm also working through the truth that, as I come out about being non-binary, the world around me keeps going through a deeper transformation than I am. People I've known for a long time are suddenly stiff around me when they used to be breezy. Friends ask me questions like, "I know you use new pronouns, but that's just for the public, right? I don't have to use your new pronouns, do I?" Now, my longest-standing lover and dominant is telling me I can cash in on my small vagina because it holds value for cis men—even though that's not a job I've expressed interest in.

When Evie and I were two bisexual women who got together every so often for BDSM, there was an air of mutual respect for each other's lives—Evie as a globe-trotting pro dom moving through a divorce, and me as a depressed cubicle worker with dreams of bright lights and Broadway. As hackneyed and unlikely as my Broadway dreams were back then, Evie didn't offer me career input.

I can't separate the changes in how I'm articulating my gender from the economic precarity in my new career, and I can't separate those from the swift changes I'm witnessing in how people treat me. When I try to separate these factors, it feels like solving a Rubik's Cube that's working against being solved. I can't get anywhere. All I know is that friends, colleagues, and lovers used to expect me to succeed in my ambitions, and now they don't.

Lucy sits down next to Evie and unzips her fire-engine-red PVC dress, exposing her tits and cunt. She looks her fluffer in the eyes, snaps her fingers, and points at her own cunt. There's nothing unclear about the instruction.

The fluffer gets on their knees between Lucy's legs and smothers her cunt with their face. Lucy puts her hand on the fluffer's head, pushing their face deeper into her clit, and closes her eyes, keeping a firm grip on the back of their skull.

Maybe Evie, Lucy, and the fluffer are having a great time, but I can't see the world through any other eyes than the ones I have, and at this moment, what I see annoys me.

I don't like the fluffer's passivity and namelessness. I don't like that we're two trans people, but the fluffer doesn't to want to interact with me, so I can't check if they're okay—or if both of us are being treated the way we deserve to be.

I don't like Lucy's snapping and pointing, or Evie's offer that I get penetrated by small penises.

I don't like the look in Evie's eyes as she looks from the fluffer down on their knees over to me. She knows better than to snap her fingers, but I can tell what's on her mind because it's written all over her face. She's not a person to accidentally betray what she's thinking.

For a moment, I think about doing it and picture it: Evie and her bestie, sitting side by side on a sofa in a sex club, getting head from two little trans masc enbies.

It feels like such a bizarre replication and recasting of misogynistic tropes that I can't handle it.

When Evie and I have gone to fetish parties together before, we've laughed at the ego-driven rope guys who promise to make women popular on FetLife as long as they can get a blow job. We've joked about how toxic those guys are, how much we hate them, and how they're pathetic aspiring pimps.

We've talked about being wild, free, and imaginative together through kink, and how, when practiced personally as opposed to professionally, kink is a way to subvert the existing power dynamics of society in order to imagine other ways of being.

Did I really come out as a queer person, a kinky person, and a non-binary person only to watch frat bro culture get re-enacted by queer high femmes?

I don't want to give head on command because another enby is giving head on command.

I didn't want to play fluffer for straight dudes when I thought I was cisgender. Now that I know myself better than that, I don't want to be the trans fluffer for hot cis women, either.

I don't even want to be the person who *has* a fluffer. I didn't come out about being trans masculine to embrace the gross codes society attaches to masculinity. Gender roles, gendered power dynamics, and hierarchies of power related to whose gender has more privilege—I'm so tired of all of it. It's boring, and I'm choking on the boredom. I didn't come out to keep engaging with a damaging system from a different vantage point. I don't want to have power over anyone or let anyone to have power over me.

My cunt is getting wet, because that's what happens in my body when I feel threatened—but this is not the kind of sex or bottoming I'm into.

"I'm going to go get off," I say to Evie.

I say it to her coldly, like it's a slap in the face.

I walk away from the three of them and over to the where the Sybian is set up onstage. By the good grace of some non-binary God, there isn't a line for it. The staff running the Sybian station already have cling wrap on hand. Other people must have been asking to make Sybian condoms out of cling wrap too.

I choose the Sybian attachment I want to place on the saddle— a non-penetrative layer of soft sucker pads that will vibrate once the Sybian's turned on and rub along the outside of me. I wrap the whole saddle in cling wrap and hose down the sucker pads with lube.

"Do you want to hold the control for the Sybian and change the speeds yourself? Or do you want to direct me, and I'll decrease or increase the intensity?" a staff person asks.

"You work the dial, please. I just want to be free."

"We'll get you there, honey."

I climb on.

In collaboration with the staff person, I ride the Sybian like I need to, loud and ugly.

I don't want anyone to desire me, exploit me, play with pretending to exploit me, or put Baby in a corner. It feels like being loud, ugly, and kind of scary will be my protection.

I'm riding the Sybian in a way that is not pleasurable in a traditional sense. What I need, at this moment, is more about staking a claim and taking up space.

I fill the room with sounds and movements that never make their way into pornography because they are not sexy.

I growl, grunt, and come, angry, loud, pissed off, sweat-drenched, with guttural screaming.

I climb off the Sybian, Jell-O-legged.

I am cold from sweating, expunged of the worst of my rage, and relieved enough to start feeling bad about how quick I was to get angry. Goosebumps form peaks and valleys of guilt all over my body. Evie's standing at the foot of the stage, toy bag in hand, looking up at me.

"Come play with me?" she asks.

I nod, put my hands on her shoulders, and she lifts me off the stage.

She carries me to Fountain's dungeon room.

She pulls a strap-on harness out of her bag, gets on her knees, and I step into it like a kid being dressed for the day.

She slips a big glass cock into the harness's O-ring and tightens the harness around my waist.

She walks me to the Saint Andrew's cross that's a permanent fixture in the Fountain dungeon room, and I lean back into the X shape of it, my arms stretched out above my head and my legs spread-eagled. She takes rope out of her bag and ties me into the crossbeams.

She pulls a riding crop out of her bag. She slaps the inside of my outstretched thighs with it and then hits the glass cock with it. I shudder, shake, and feel my cunt lubricating all over again—only now I'm getting wet because Evie whacking at my glass cock feels good.

Evie notices the reaction.

She steps close, places her leg between my outstretched thighs, and knees me in my glass cock and cunt.

The feeling is intense, thudding, and shockingly delicious.

I squint. I'm not usually into thud pain. Evie always shows me what I don't know about myself. My eyes get bleary. My mouth hangs open.

I feel so good, having Evie knee me over and over in the place where, in some parallel universe, I have balls. It's rawer than being her toilet. Evie's knee grinding into my cock and cunt is direct and blunt. I'm open, safe, and wilfully ready to be this vulnerable. Our play is primal and consensual. My anger about the nameless fluffer and the way two femmes treated them hasn't completely subsided, though. There's still a tension in me that needs release. An impulse rises up in me suddenly. My subspace brain goes somewhere it's never gone before. While I still seek consent, I don't care enough about Evie in this moment to just push my impulse away.

"Can I shout a string of obscenities at you?" I ask.

"Yes."

"Can they be misogynistic and disgusting?"

"I've been called worse by clients, I'm sure."

She steps back from me and kicks at my cunt and glass cock with her leather boot. The thud into my body is even deeper.

I scream at her every degrading, insulting, repugnant name imaginable, unleashed from somewhere deep in my psyche.

I scream at her words I've never used before, phrases I didn't know I was carrying inside me, and images of shame.

Evie stops kicking me.

My vision is fuzzy and blurred. Even so, I see the easy stillness of her face crack and reveal what's underneath.

She looks completely defeated.

For a moment, I see an Evie I've never seen before: an Evie whose heartbreak can't be cauterized with coke, an Evie who grew up having everything except safety, and an Evie who is actually hurt by what happens, even when she's the one throwing the punches.

I know her better in this moment than I've known in her our years of being play partners.

I wish I could hold her. I wish could have sent her shit-show, rich monster father to jail.

I wish I could show her where I've been so she could see that the reason I deal in pain in my intimate life is because pain is most of what I've known.

I wish I could show her that even though we're no longer the same gender, I haven't forgotten what it means to be a cis woman in this world, too often having to choose between financial security and autonomy.

I wish we could both experience being ourselves in this world without the world beating us down and compromising who we can be.

Her mask of impassivity snaps back on, and she goes back to kicking me, in a way that's controlled but hard.

She kicks me in my cock, cunt, and soul.

I wordlessly, gutturally scream again.

She smothers my scream with her lips.

I realize I'm crying as I feel my tears on her face.

There's a difference between being useful and being used. Maybe the fluffer is happy being snapped at and directed—I can hold space for that reality. Role-playing with power dynamics can be fun and healing when that's what someone is into.

I can't hold space for Evie looking from the fluffer to me, from one trans person to another trans person, like she's a cis dude at a college party whose buddy's already getting a blow job, so she expects one too.

Just because we're queer fetishists doesn't mean we're always subverting harmful norms.

Sometimes we're internalizing fucked-up behaviours and power dynamics and re-enacting them thoughtlessly, out of instinct, due to conditioning, and in self-defence rather than from a place of care, compassion, and self-awareness.

That's certainly what I was doing when I screamed misogynistic obscenities at Evie.

In the fetish I explore, I want to be reinvented in ways that surprise me, where I'm the clay, my dominant is the sculptor, and we're collaborating. In that state of reinvention, I've made discoveries about my gender, I've found the will to chase my dreams, and I've been able to look life's hard questions in the face and ask myself: what does a life that's really mine look like, and what's really a life worth living? Evie has been such a significant part of that journey, and I've seen how happy the intuition and freedom in our play has made her on days other than today.

I hate seeing her look defeated as much as I hate feeling pressured to fall in line.

I'm let down by her, disappointed in myself, and dehydrated.

I understand Evie better now that I've seen what's beneath her stillness and composure—but there's no way to express that to her without creating more distance. There's so much hanging in the air between us but no way to put it into words.

The language and roles in kink are a clumsy tool we use to try to find out who we are and convey that. Because they're clumsy tools, sometimes we get confused and tripped up by the shortfalls of the roles, the language, and our own uninterrogated assumptions.

Evie unties me from the Saint Andrew's cross. We sit on the floor together without speaking. Lucy brings us a couple of bottles of water.

Evie doesn't ask me why I hurled a string of obscenities at her, and I don't offer an explanation.

ROPE IS BULLSHIT

"Maybe next time, the three of us can play at my place," Leah
offers.

I'm at a small but publicly advertised BDSM event in a warehouse just south of downtown Toronto. The warehouse has been
subdivided into work-live-play studios, and the unit next door is
hosting a goth metal party. Because it's Toronto in February and
no one wants slush dragged inside, both the kink and goth metal
events are socks only. In the vestibule between them, there's a
bizarre assortment of various pairs of shoes, strewn haphazardly,
like a miniature mountain range of colliding economic brackets
and life priorities. Anyone who has left expensive footwear here
risks having it stolen, leaving them to tiptoe through the snow
in socks and nylons to their Uber later on. The warehouse is on
the edge of where new housing developments meet the industrial
areas of the shoreline that haven't been gentrified yet, but will be.
Getting here, I followed the blue dot on the map on my phone,
turning off familiar streets into an area where the sidewalks
disappear, where the lighting at night is limited, and where no
one can hear you scream. I've arrived alone.

Small but publicly advertised BDSM events can be dicey. Usually there are enough lifestyle tourists there to make things presumptuous and dangerous—tourists who have seen *Fifty Shades of Grey* and *Secretary* and have adopted these films as meaningful kink playbooks. At the same time, often too few reliable and experienced players turn up to create the critical mass of courage and goodwill needed to shut down unacceptable conduct. I have no idea who owns this space, but taking it in, I can make assumptions.

It's an open-concept, two-level studio. If someone lives here, they live a 24-7 kink lifestyle. There are spanking benches, a wall of canes, and hardpoints in the ceiling for rope suspension—but there's no love, affection, or care present in the objects here. Unlike James's rope salon, this studio feels neglected. Everything's bashed in, scuffed up, and devoid of humour. If Costco sold BDSM equipment, that's where this place would have been outfitted by. The second level overlooks the first, and on it there's a swinger-sized Jacuzzi tub alongside a large scummy fish tank which, despite being full of water, contains no fish. The one bathroom in the studio is clad in imitation-wood panelling, and the bathroom door purposefully doesn't lock. It adds to a general air of discomfort and depression that permeates the space, as you contemplate using the toilet, knowing anyone could walk in on you at any moment.

Whoever owns this studio, it's likely a cishet guy, possibly with untreated anxiety, and he probably overcompensates for his anxiety by exerting control. Whoever this guy is, he'd probably describe any women he plays with as his possessions. Way too often in fetish circles, you run into cishet guys who have turned a modest amount of equity into a foothold in community relevance. The rest of us put up with the presence of these moderately wealthy and highly problematic guys because they fund a lot of the public BDSM scene.

There's no door charge to get into this event, and all alcohol here is free. Between the imitation wood, the dinginess, the lack of bathroom privacy, and the general predatory vibe, this might be the least sexy fetish event I've ever been to.

Because this event is publicly advertised on FetLife and doesn't require an invitation or a personal connection to get into, it's very straight. A fetish event usually has to be exclusive to queer people, exclusive to women and trans folks, or require being vouched for to get in to avoid being inundated with cisgender heterosexuality.

On the other side of downtown, James is throwing a play party at the Shibari Salon, which he said I was welcome to come to if I wanted. I've arrived at this party instead because it's Saturday night, I have FOMO, and I don't want James to be my sole source for getting tied. He's likely leaving Canada soon, and unless I'm willing to drop the emotional role rope bondage plays in my life, I should be putting myself in positions where I might meet a new rigger—even if that means coming to events where I don't fit in. I'm sad that James, my friend and rope top, is moving on. I channel that sadness into looking for my next rope fix.

I scan the party, looking for anything I can connect to. Any cis guy here on his own is not my best bet, safetywise—which rules out most of the people here. I walk around the party with blinders on, because most single guys at fetish events take any form of eye contact as an invitation for conversation. Couples are a safer bet. There are no queer couples here, so I scan the women with men. I look to a woman's mood and demeanour as an indicator of safety. If she looks happy and self-assured, I take it as a sign that the guy she's with isn't dangerous. If she looks blitzed on drugs, in a constant state of being triggered, or if she can't take her eyes off the floor in front of her, I take it as a red flag that she's in an abusive relationship masquerading as dom/sub play.

All the assumptions I bring to what I'm seeing could be incorrect, but when you go to straight fetish events on your own, you get used to the politics of those spaces, the kinds of people you meet there, and over time you develop a set of filters. I could be wrong about what I'm picking up on when I meet a submissive who is quiet and withdrawn, but if I'm right, I'm at risk of being abused too.

I'm about to leave and either drop by the Salon or head home to eat shawarma in bed when I notice another AFAB person who has shown up alone.

She's kneeling on the floor in frilly ankle socks, pastel-gingham underwear, and an undershirt. She's colouring in a colouring book with pencil crayons. The aesthetics of the images she's colouring in are cartoony, but the images themselves are of campy kink: big-nippled breasts bursting out of bras, spanking scenes with wide eyes and big, round, open mouths, and lots of femme-on-femme bondage. It's the height of the adult colouring book fad, as Millennials across North America grapple with the fact that they're skilled and educated enough to be adults but don't want to grow up, so I've seen a lot of adult colouring books lately. This is the first one I've thought was hilarious.

"Your colouring book is adorable."

She looks up at me. The tone of her voice is purposefully infantilized. She's engaged in a bit of solo little play. I've never seen a little out in the world without a big.

"What's your name?"

"I'm Sly."

"That's a state of being, not a name."

"You're adorable."

"You wanna colour with me, Sly?"

I kneel down next to the little. The cold floor turns my kneecaps pink on contact, sprouting goosebumps along my ass and the back of my legs. I lean forward in this cold, unfriendly fetish party, reach for a red pencil crayon, and start colouring in some big, pouty lips.

The colouring book owner introduces herself as Vanessa.

Slowly and quietly, with an affected childishness, she tells me about all the adult facts of her life. She's in her twenties, and she's a student at the University of Toronto. She loves anime, hates her family, and is taking biology so she can make enough money to get away from everyone. She's bisexual and a bottom. The facts she states are simple, to the point, and direct, but she delivers them with a singsong, upward-inflected voice and with an effortless delight, like a kid talking about what just happened on *Sesame Street*.

Littles are a wonderful part of the BDSM scene; there's nothing more charming than a wilful, expressive little.

Just as submissives are complemented by dominants, littles are often complemented by bigs. Being a little is a form of age play, where an adult person acts like someone much younger, anything from an infant to a teenager. Sometimes a little's persona is simply a younger version of their real self, and sometimes it's a made-up personality. Sometimes both bigs and littles can have different gender identities than the gender they live in every day. For littles, there can be a fair amount of performativity to the role, including having toys—like a colouring book and pencil crayons—that are specific to being in little headspace. For some, this form of role play also includes adopting younger mannerisms and wearing different clothes. A lot of littles enjoy attention—whether it's positive attention for being good, rewards for making discoveries, or negative attention in the form of punishments for misbehaving. The simple need to be nurtured, through both encouragement and discipline, is part of what makes being a little, and age play, satisfying.

Age play can involve some form of sex, but it doesn't always. Whether sex is integrated or not, age play, like a lot of BDSM, can be gratifying because it's a means to escape the pressures, stressors, and responsibilities of being an adult—which is why it isn't about fetishizing children. Instead, it's about enjoying attention without having responsibilities, enjoying protection without having to live up to expectations, and being respected without the burden of having to earn respect.

Whether the term used is "baby girl," "brat," or another kink moniker, littles can be any gender, and age play can be a way to live out the fantasy of experiencing unconditional care.

On the floor with Vanessa, I sink into my little headspace too. My little is quieter and shyer than I usually am—or maybe my little is a version of me without the masks of extroversion I've developed as an adult in order to keep the introverted person that I actually am safe.

As a little, I like listening more than I like talking. I like having something to do—like colouring—so that I am distracted from how I'm being perceived. I like being near others and watching them, but I don't like making eye contact. I stick my tongue out and grasp it lightly with my teeth, like I did instinctively as a kid whenever I was concentrating on a task, before being picked on at school bullied me out of my own self-soothing habits.

In little headspace, I'm very aware of sensory details: the weight of the pencil crayon between my fingers, the size of my hands in relation to objects. I don't worry about the larger picture of life because I'm drowning in the textures, temperatures, sounds, and shapes of the moment. Little headspace is a state of openness and being present, a state where frustrations, anger, and old grudges covering old wounds don't really exist. I kneel on the floor, listen to Vanessa's ongoing kidlike monologue, and give a cartoon drawing of a fierce femmedom some blue teeth.

Most of the guys at the studio don't really know what to do with the two of us, babbling on the floor and colouring, so they leave us be. A spanking bench near us frees up, and Vanessa and I decide to do a little-on-little spanking scene. Vanessa climbs on top of the bench, and I spank her little bum softly. The spanking isn't intense or particularly satisfying for either of us sexually, but it's a silly little thing two silly littles can share. We aren't hot for each other—we're both bottoms, and bottom/bottom relationships don't usually work. Neither of us is getting off on the other, but we do both feel a faith in people restored—which we both need to feel at a kink party as dismal and depressing as this one. We're both at this event to have unmet needs met. We aren't the right fit to meet each other's needs, but at least by sharing in being littles, we feel less alone.

Vanessa packs up her pencil crayons, changes back into her street clothes, and suddenly I wouldn't be able to pick her out of a crowd of STEM students on the subway. Her little drops away. We hug goodbye and don't exchange contact information. Neither of us needs to pretend we have a connection that's bigger than it is.

While we've been on our own as littles, the party has gotten much bigger and busier.

I look over the railing of the second floor at the party below, which is now standing room only. In the centre of a sea of mostly straight men, a rigger and a rope bottom are setting up to do a scene.

I recognize the rigger, even though the last time I saw him, he looked like a farm boy, dressed in denim overalls and a white wifebeater while he tied someone onstage at the Black Mask Bondage Extravaganza.

He's a cishet guy in his thirties with a round, young-looking face. He's got blond hair in tight little curls and wears his hair just long enough that it inherently wants to be ruffled. He has light-brown eyes, with a faint dusting of freckles across his nose and cheeks. In the rope scene, he goes by the name Broadsword, and the rope bottom he's with goes by the name Dagger. I know this because at the BMBE, Broadsword was handing out business cards he'd had printed for his pseudo-professional life as an aspiring dominant for hire.

Dagger, his rope bottom, is also cisgender and in her late twenties. She has porcelain-white skin, dark eyes, and straight, shoulder-length brown-black hair. All of her features are made up to stand out against her skin: dark eyeliner, red-black nails, dark-red lips, and dark-red-and-black underwear. The contrast is so strong that she'd look like a doll if it weren't for the cellulite that carves little rivulets into her body below her hips. She looks like someone who is trying to be compelling and accomplishing it—but she also looks like she's fumbling to figure out how to look her age, with so much makeup caked that on that it ages her. Her lingerie looks like it was picked up under deep markdown because the style is from two seasons ago.

They're an odd couple—Broadsword a man-boy clambering to turn rope into a source of income, and Dagger a young woman who seems out of sync with her own youth.

I'm always drawn to people who stand out in strange ways.

Even though I'm not engaged in little play anymore, I still feel more open and receptive than when I arrived. My guards are lowered because the openness and receptiveness that comes with being a little dissipates gradually. I head downstairs and loiter around the rope scene, pushing through the standing-room-only crowd that's gathered around the two of them. Dagger dangles in rope from the ceiling while Broadsword huffs around her, unty-ing her and retying her through the choreography of their staged suspension scene.

I catch Broadsword's eye as I sit on the floor near their scene. The rest of the crowd is mostly cis guys who have donned fetish dress code and are hovering, wanting, watching, and wishing they could fuck Dagger. I'm wearing crew socks, a tie-dyed T-shirt, and lime-green briefs, so I stand out visually. I stand out energetically too, because unlike the crowd of straight guys around me, I'm watching him instead of watching her.

"Let's talk later," Broadsword mouths at me.

They wrap up their scene. Broadsword takes a bow. Dagger dances around the room, receiving compliments and adoration while eye-fucking every cis man in the place. She seems to love attention, and Broadsword doesn't seem to mind—which is a good sign. I take it to mean that he is probably is a safe dude to play with, because Dagger appears to be happy and her own person.

The studio's owner steps forward to pay Broadsword for the rope performance. He lives up to my assumptions of who owns this studio: he's a cishet dude, and he fluctuates between degrading and flattering whoever he's speaking to, in a self-serving cycle of cutting people down so they're vulnerable enough to need his validation. He's loud, self-impressed, and has long white-grey hair and a long grey beard like a forlorn wizard crossed with an angry, aging narcissist. As he approaches Broadsword, he's got two women with him, both scantily clad. The women look like shells of their former selves. They're collared and leashed, and the studio owner holds their leashes tightly in his fist. I throw up in my mouth a little, waiting until he's done talking to Broadsword. I don't want to be anywhere near this misogynist's orbit. The atmosphere around him and the leashed women with him is suffocating instead of fun. Looking at them, their play seems devoid of hope or desire.

I worry about these women with the studio owner, looking at their exposed breasts, their slumped shoulders, the bruises on their thighs, and the fact that they never look up or speak—even though I've joyfully donned similar sets of bruises from my own play scenes. There's a difference between dom/sub dynamics and people who seem beaten down, like they've given up. The pain and struggle in BDSM are a mechanism as opposed to an end point. The more BDSM venues I venture into, though, the more I run into dominants like this, for whom pain and control are the end point and preying on underlying trauma seems to be the mechanism. I meet a lot of smart people through fetish, and at some point, a lot of these smart people seem to conspicuously ignore real predatory behaviour in the scene.

The studio owner hands Broadsword a stack of twenties.

I catch Broadsword's eye again as he stuffs the money into his pocket. While Dagger schmoozes up a storm, Broadsword and I start talking.

In rope they might be Broadsword and Dagger, but in real life they're Noah and Leah. Leah is a Toronto-based Canadian camgirl with a few in-person clients she does sounding sessions for. Noah is an American customer service representative who lives in Ann Arbor. He talks in a way that is sweet, though a little domineering, but he also comes across like an open book. The openness with which he talks about his life and his relationship with Dagger is inviting and disarming. When he isn't tying for pay or for fun, his main passion is LARPing—live-action role-playing.

"Like with the medieval costumes and stuff, in public?"

"That's where I got the name Broadsword from."

"I thought maybe Broadsword referred to anatomy."

"I wish. I mean, wait, yeah no, it's about my big dick. I have a big dick."

"What's going on here?" Leah asks as she slides next to Noah.

"Leah, this is Sly. She's a newish rope bunny here in Toronto."

"Any pronoun used with respect works for me, but if you can, I prefer them and they."

"I should have asked, and I'm sorry. Leah, this is Sly, and *they're* kind of new in the rope scene. Sly, I use he and him pronouns, and Leah uses she and her. I'm a rigger—you know that—but Leah's also getting into tying too."

Leah and I shake hands. She looks at me like she could make me jizz with her eyelashes.

"Your eyes are fucking amazing."

"They come in handy for camming. And for seducing little cuties," she says.

She whispers in Noah's ear and flits off to schmooze again.

"Sly, are you of flexible sexual orientation, by any chance?"

"I'm bi."

"Leah and I have been hoping to find a pet we could share."

"Who says I would want to be your pet?"

"No one. But that begs the question—would you want to be?"

Noah's in town for another couple of days before he has to get back to his day job in Michigan. He and I plan for the three of us to connect at Fountain the next day, at around eleven o'clock in the morning, when the sex club opens. It's public, neutral ground, cheaper than a hotel room, and meeting there doesn't necessarily make rope the foregone conclusion, but it leaves the door open for it.

"You know, I almost left this party before the two of you got here. If I hadn't stumbled across a little a few hours ago, I'd be home in bed already."

"Where's that little gone? Bring her to Fountain too," Noah says.

The next morning, I'm at the sex club, carrying a tray of three Starbucks coffees. I've been spending more and more of my nights and weekends at Fountain, as if looking for the meaning of life through sex has become my part-time profession. This morning at Fountain, it's as if I'm on a blind date, at an unexpected work meeting, and looking for a new, reliable drug hookup all at once.

I sip my coffee and hope Noah will bring rope. I hope I get to know Leah better. I hope that Noah's cishetness continues to exist in a behavioural range that is tolerable. I think about the fact that I've never been tied by two people before. The idea of a loving couple co-tying me turns me on. My hair is still wet from my morning shower, and my deodorant, gummy from being applied while I was damp, sticks my shirt to my skin. The turn-around time, from last night to now, has been quick. I'm not exactly keeping up with myself. I'm not thinking very hard about what I'm doing.

Eleven in the morning on a Sunday at Fountain, the place is mostly full of senior swingers. They're lovely, friendly, and body positive—it's like visiting a retirement nudist colony. The Beatles are playing over Fountain's speakers.

Noah arrives first on his own. Leah had a client thing, he tells me, and she's on her way. We're the youngest people at Fountain by a mile. We bond over how much we're fish out of water. Noah offers that he's always been called chubby, so he knows how to enjoy life, even in situations where he doesn't feel welcome.

He's grateful and surprised that I've brought him and Leah coffees. We both have a nervous and excited energy. We're being ourselves, but also trying to impress each other. I hold my posture straight instead of crumbling around my chest to conceal my breasts the way I usually do. Noah gets embarrassed and laughs at himself when he spills coffee on his chin. I ask to ruffle the tiniest bit of snow out of his curls. We've both hustled to be here.

I've never had a healthy relationship modelled for me, so I think it's a positive sign when people want to lavish a lot of attention on me very quickly.

Leah arrives at the club, kisses Noah hello on the lips, and kisses me on my cheek. Her mouth lands very close to my mouth, so that the crease of her lips overlaps mine. It's better than a full kiss on my mouth would have been because it leaves me wanting.

"Hello, champion," she says to me.

"Leah, Sly brought us coffee."

"I saw from your text."

"Isn't that nice?"

"I've already had coffee today," Leah says.

She spots someone she knows—which is surprising, given the age demographic here. She flies off to socialize like she did at the BDSM studio. Noah and I sit at the bar together with our three coffees. We share the last one, swapping saliva on the cup rim.

Leah flits in and out of our conversation, darting in to be flattering and charming and darting out again just as quickly, while Noah sits and builds a rapport with me.

"Have I done something to piss Leah off?"

"No, not at all. She's just shyer than you'd think, and she doesn't switch out of work mode very easily. She's always networking. When I met her, she was homeless, in and out of shelters, and her face was just riddled with acne. I helped her see how beautiful she is and how she could use her beauty. Don't worry, when we're done talking, I'll wrangle her."

I don't tend to press people for more details than they readily offer, so I don't ask Noah what he means about helping her to use her beauty. It leaves me with the impression that he's helped shape her career as a camgirl and part-time sex worker. The Broadsword and Dagger dynamic is confusing. I feel drawn to them and have no judgment for their professional hustles, but I also feel destabilized by the way they behave, as individuals and toward each other. Maybe long-term kink relationships are complicated. Maybe mixing sex life and work life as a couple is *really* complicated—with Leah camming and doing sounding sessions for some in-person clients and her and Noah doing rope performances. Maybe Noah's a part-time pimp. Maybe they're nice people and just having a fight, but still rallying to show up at this the moment.

Noah asks if I'd like to go to one of the play spaces upstairs to see how some rope feels.

"Leah would like to tie you," he tells me.

On the third floor of Fountain, the three of us crawl into a padded sex cubby built into a wall and lined with purple-vinyl padding. I mention that I may have some residual little left in me from my colouring session the night before. Leah gets excited.

"You're a little, too?" she asks.

"I'm a lot of things."

Her vocal tone shifts immediately.

"My daddy's teaching me to tie up my cute friends," she says. "Do you want Daddy to show me how to tie you? Because you're cute!"

Her swift swing into little space catches me off guard, both drawing me in, turning me on, and destabilizing me—again. She's been an aloof, social sexpot over the few hours I've known her. Now suddenly she's looking me in the eye and offering me her little, instead of trying to be some stock character femme fatale. Most different of all, now she's giving me all her focus.

Leah's little persona is oriented around a daughter-fucks-daddy and daughter-helps-daddy-fuck-her-friends scenario, like the details of a sickening news headline.

In some ways, the bold and ugly horror of this role-play scenario is what makes it a turn-on, because it confronts a situation that on some level, a lot of people fear falling prey to. It's a role-play scenario that hits me in my junk and makes me wet because of the kind of sexual abuse that was inherent in my family's history—and it's the kind of situation I could have fallen into in real life when I was a kid sitting in the school library, having internet creeps ask if they could meet up with me.

Growing up in the homes and environments I did, sexual abuse felt like an inevitability. From my time in therapy, I know that one of the times I get wet is when I feel threatened, because my body is preparing itself to endure less physical harm through lubrication in the event that an assault does happen. Living my whole childhood assuming that at some point I would be raped nibbled and gnawed at the edges of my mind, leaving me feeling like I was always under threat and never safe.

On this Sunday afternoon at Fountain, however, the three of us are all here of our own will. We're all adults, and consent is being sought. It's a sex game, not real-world reality. My body perceives a threat, as Leah's little reminds me of my personal history, but I'm no longer a kid. Perceiving danger and proving that the danger isn't actually there feels good because of my inter-generational trauma and post-traumatic stress. It's healing to feel fear and then prove to myself that there was nothing to be afraid of. It's only healing, however, if the threat perceived isn't actually a present threat.

"I'm still teaching her to tie, but don't worry, I'll make sure she doesn't do any damage," Noah offers.

"Yes, please. I want to play with you and your daddy," my little answers.

"And you want my daddy's penis to wear a hat during our play?" Leah asks.

"Yes, please."

Leah ties me, and Noah guides. To say that Leah is getting into tying is a bit of an overstatement: she's really bad at rope. I don't mind because I always feel close to people when I see them vulnerable. Witnessing Leah fumble at fetish while she works hard to be a big shot in the local rope scene is an intimacy I didn't expect. Dagger's no femme fatale—she's just faking it until she makes it. The surprise of seeing past Leah's facades, her little, our age play, and Noah's big draw me in. I slip into a state of sensory overwhelm.

Leah's on her back, and every part of me leans into her cunt.

I lick just above her clit so that it doesn't go numb, while my middle and index fingers drum gently but consistently into her G spot so she can come over and over.

Noah's upright on his knees behind me, and he jackhammers into my cunt. There's still rope tied around my hips—he tugs me into him and fucks me harder.

I can feel her pleasure, his abandon, and I can feel how together they are in this moment, even though they aren't touching. I feel like I'm part of something bigger than myself, part of a relationship that predates me—because I am.

In this way, in the midst of our fucking, with my face a slave to Leah's cunt and with Noah's pelvis and stomach slamming into my ass, I feel like I'm part of a family.

After we fuck, I lie on purple-vinyl padding, covered in our sex gunk, with Noah's knotted-up used condom on my hip. He and Leah are sitting on either side of me, and I'm looking up at them.

Noah asks me to teach him how to eat pussy.

"You're clearly better at it than me," he says.

I can hear him and can respond appropriately in context, but I'm miles away.

For a moment, space and time fold, and I'm actually a little kid now, in a bed somewhere. I'm part of a family that accepts, understands, and takes care of one another, with two caring adults looking down at me and loving me. It's my bedtime, they're here, and I'm safe.

It's not a real memory I have or a scene that ever happened. My parents hated each other and only loved me in as much as they could use me to hurt each other. I have no memory of them being in the same place at the same time without fighting.

Space and time have folded to a parallel universe where as a kid I got to experience what a sense of security, predictability, and reliability felt like. Our sloppy rope scene, our little-on-little-on-big age play, and our fucking produce a profound moment of personal calm and well-being.

Instinctively, my situation with this couple isn't about getting my next rope fix anymore. What I see when I look up at them has almost nothing to do with rope and almost everything to do with the fantasy of being loved unconditionally.

Endorphins run wild through me from the strain of being tied, and dopamine hits me hard from the sex, the age play, and the relief of perceiving a threat in the two of them, then proving to myself that it was a false alarm. I'm okay. I'm better than okay. Somehow, in this odd couple, maybe I've stumbled across the kind of kink relationship that could grow and evolve into something that I might one day describe as chosen family.

"Maybe next time, the three of us can play at my place," Leah offers.

It's weeks before Noah is able to make it up from Ann Arbor again. Even though Leah and I both live in Toronto, she doesn't offer to stay in touch while Noah's unavailable, or to see me without him present.

Noah, on the other hand, texts me constantly.

His texts arrive from where he's working at a call centre in Michigan while I'm in my cubicle in North York. I figure that maybe the reason Noah and I talk but Leah and I don't is that both Noah and I have day lives that are miles away from the people we want to be. He texts me concept drawings for costumes he wants for his LARPing, sketches of rope scenes he wants to play out, and photos of the lunches he's packed for himself each weekday.

In between these anecdotal shares, he keeps up his daddy age play with me.

I'm going to thrust my big daddy dick inside you and ejaculate so hard that my come will flood your cervix and you'll get pregnant and then I'll make sex slaves out of our little babies.

I lock the stall door in my office's bathroom, lift my feet off the floor so none of my co-workers can find me, and jerk off to Noah's texts.

Like with the age play we played out in person, it's the disgusting, exploitative nature of Noah's text messages that makes them arousing. Icky enough to feel familiar to my life and family history, his texts skim the surface of my trauma just enough for me to keep feeling a sense of threat. I keep emerging from the bathroom stall, post-jerk off, feeling like I've debunked the sense of threat through our play, and that as a result, my trauma no longer holds sway over me. It's kind of pathetic to be hiding in the bathroom at my suburban office job, jerking off to age play texts from an almost stranger, but it makes me feel seen, and it gives me reprieve from grief and boredom, so I don't care.

Outside of work, I hang out with James at the Shibari Salon as much as possible even though the fact he's leaving is an overwhelming part of what I'm grieving.

I watch James try to come to terms with the fact that he has to give up the sleazy, slutty life he's built for himself here in Canada due to visa constraints. He has the soul of a perpetual five-year-old, and like a kid, part of him is completely accepting of change while another part of him is in complete denial about it. He chain-smokes and eats a bag of sugar-coated gummy worms for dinner while he slowly says goodbye to his home. I sit naked on the tatami flooring of the Shibari Salon and, in my heart, I try to slowly say goodbye to him.

I soak in the details of the Salon as much as I can as I start an internal countdown on the dwindling number of times I'll see him grinning as he opens the door, pulls me off the street, and pulls me into his world of pushing the edges of what's possible. I'm saying goodbye to something that's bigger than a man, because Sakura and his Shibari Salon have become my inspiration for living.

I run my fingers along the inscriptions on the wall by the door of the Salon, written by all the people who have tied and been tied here. I'm part of a large demographic of dreamers who have dangled inside the Salon's timber rib cage. I hear James's voice in my ears from the first time I was here.

"That's the yearbook, sweetie."

Dagger's name is in the yearbook, under my fingers.

"I didn't get a chance to tell you. I fucked Dagger and Broadsword the other day."

"Really? Broadsword's your type?" James asks.

"What do you mean?"

"I can't stand being around him and Dagger. I can't listen to their constant bickering."

"I guess I haven't noticed."

"Watch yourself, Sly, yeah? Broadsword doesn't have a good reputation in the scene."

"In what way?"

"He's not been great with consent, according to some."

"But you know him and are friends with him?"

"He wants to get better at rope and is willing to pay. I don't need the people who pay me to know what I think of them."

It's the first time James shows any concern about my sex life.

We've been open and encouraging of each other's sensual experiences, so I don't know what to make of his warning, especially so close to him no longer being in this fetish scene anymore. It's hard for me to take advice that isolates me from new connections when I'm already losing the connection that means the most to me.

Noah comes back to Toronto and quickly invites me over Leah's Liberty Village condo to pick up our play where we left off. When I arrive, Leah hasn't made it back yet from a session with a client. Noah answers the door. His fingers are stained purple from prepping beets for a borscht he's making.

"You're making borscht for your group sex date night? Actually?"

"Sly, who says soup can't be sexy? Open your mind, girl."

"I don't like being called a girl."

"Right, I remember you said that last time. They and them. I validate you. I see you."

We make conversation while beets bubble on the stove. Noah shows me a meme that's making the FetLife rounds; it's regarding consent, using a teacup analogy.

"See, the point it's making is that if you ask someone if they want a cup of coffee and they say yes, but then you serve them a cup of tea, you haven't respected their consent, because you haven't brought them the thing they said yes to."

"Yeah, Noah—I'm not the target audience for this meme. I already know how consent works."

Noah's put off by my reaction. I feel bad. Maybe he's trying to indicate that his consent-breaching ways are in the past?

Our relationship is too young and casual for me to clarify while also already being too layered and complicated to feel easy.

If I didn't have so many unmet emotional needs, I'd leave, because new relationships should be easier than this one is—but I do have a lot of unmet emotional needs, so I stay.

Noah switches gears and starts telling me about a new rope bunny named Esther he's starting to play with in Ann Arbor. He says Leah likes her too. It's a bit of a clapback, for me shutting down Noah's virtue signalling, but I roll with it.

He pulls out his phone to share photos of Esther from her FetLife profile, images of her in underwear, hanging half-naked and upside down in rope, wearing Halloween costume rabbit ears. I've seen thousands of photos of cis women in the rope scene, and even so, every straight-dude dom I've ever met always wants to share photos of their conquests, as if seeing variations on the same thing over and over is thrilling. I want to be polite, so I make comments that are bland and supportive.

"Mm-hmm! A rope bunny—literally."

We talk as if we haven't been sharing disgusting texts for weeks. It occurs to me that maybe Noah's avoiding acknowledging our age play text sessions because Leah doesn't know about them and may walk in any moment. Or maybe he's ignoring it because he has sext sessions with a lot of people and has forgotten that some of them have been with me. There are just red flags all over the place.

"Esther's half-Asian, too. It's so sexy," Noah says.

"Are you fetishizing race?"

"I like what I like. That's the point of kink, isn't it?"

Leah opens to the door and walks in. It saves me from getting into it with Noah about why liking a spanking and liking people for being of a particular racial background are different things entirely.

With cis men in the fetish scene, it's hard to scope out whether they're saying the things they really think or just repeating the shitty things they've heard other shitty doms say. I want to like Noah. I want to believe that what's tumbling off his tongue is the swan song of his cis male fragility and that he's categorizing and objectifying people as a smokescreen for his own insecurities. I want to see where things go with my play sessions with him and Leah. I want two cisgender people who are popular in the fetish scene in my corner as I begin expressing that I'm not cisgender and as my life's about to change. It's hard to know if someone really is an asshole or if they just sound like an asshole. Or maybe it isn't hard to know, and I just don't want to face facts because I'm scared of the world and want companionship to make me feel less afraid.

Leah looks absolutely exhausted, sweaty, and like more sex is the last thing on her mind. I want to make her feel comfortable, but I don't know her well enough to know how to be comforting.

"Noah was telling me about your new love in Ann Arbor."

Leah looks at Noah with panic.

"I didn't use the word 'love.' I just said there's a bunny in Ann Arbor who we've started playing with."

Leah doesn't respond. The tension in the air could be cut by a knife, a broadsword, or a dagger.

"I'm sorry—that's true, Leah. Noah didn't call anyone 'love.' I was just being poetic."

Leah speaks to me without taking her eyes off Noah.

"That's okay, champion. *You* don't have to be sorry."

I think of James's comment about their bickering as I get a taste of it. I feel like a kid again—only now it's because the family around me is fighting.

This is the depressing but real downside to dating couples: sometimes you get drawn into their ongoing conflicts with each other. The two of them talk it out in Leah's kitchen in hushed tones. I eat beet soup alone in the living room, with nothing better to do than take in the details of her living space. Occasionally Noah calls over to me to ask me if I need more sour cream.

The paint on the walls of Leah's condo is chipped and scuffed, and the fixtures in the kitchen and bathroom are particleboard and laminate. There isn't much in the way of furnishings, no art or posters up on any of the walls—just a black-pleather couch, a coffee table, some kitchen bar stools, and on the second floor, a bed, a large wardrobe cabinet, and a mirror.

The condo looks like it was outfitted quickly with the stuff a straight guy picks out when he's spent too much time on 4Chan. A rope hardpoint drilled into the ceiling is the only unusual thing that's been put into the space. Since Leah's not very good at rope, I assume this hardpoint has been put in so that at some point, Noah can use Leah's home to start throwing his own private rope lessons and performances. The home feels like a commercial shell, meant to be used rather than enjoyed.

Noah and Leah come over to me from the kitchen.

"Come upstairs with us, champion?" Leah asks.

I try to shrug off their drama and follow Leah's lead. We head upstairs to the bedroom.

Things go the same way as the first time we played at Fountain. Leah tries to tie me, and Noah catches and corrects her mistakes, making sure she doesn't give me nerve damage. It's a setting where I'm not sure which one of these two people I trust more. It varies from moment to moment.

We lose most of our clothes quickly—Leah and I are naked, and Noah is in his boxers. My brain always catalogues irrelevant details during sex. I take in the shape and width of Leah's shoulders, the way Noah's tummy presses against the waistband of his boxer briefs, and the familiar smell of jute as I lie on an unfamiliar bed. Rope dust sheds from the bonds and buries my brain in the layers of the galaxy as I fall into subspace and return to all of our origins as stardust.

This is good. Rope is familiar. I can lean into this.

Leah goes to her large wardrobe cabinet and pulls out a big pink dildo and a lace-lined black panty harness. She pulls it on and slips the dildo into the O-ring of the panties. Noah lies on his back on the bed next to me, fiddling around on his phone.

"You two are so sexy. Can I take a photo of you two so I can show Esther? Just so she can see how good my life is?"

Without looking at each other, Leah and I both say no at the same time, like a slightly pissed-off chorus.

"Totally, I get it. Thank you for your boundaries. Can I take a photo of you two for myself, just to jerk off to later? You two are just so sexy."

I wait for Leah to answer. She says yes.

I look at Leah. Her femme fatale gaze evades my eyes.

My body is full of conflicting chemical responses. Consent check-ins are happening, but they're happening in rapid succession. I'm not exactly keeping up with myself or finding the space, in these fast conversations, to find what I feel—so I just keep the sex play moving.

"Okay to a photo, as long as it's kept private," I answer.

Leah wants to fuck my cunt this time. I'm game. I kneel down between Noah's outstretched legs while Leah stands upright on her knees behind me. Noah pulls his erection out of his boxers. I tell him to put on a condom. He does. I suck his dick while behind me, Leah slips her big pink dildo inside me.

I try to feel present in the sensations of the moment, because I can't feel comfortable in the social dynamics.

I close my eyes.

I can hear Leah moaning.

I can feel Noah trying to thrust his hips into my face.

I can feel the unforgiving hard silicone of Leah's dildo parting my labia. I can feel her fingers bracing on the outer edge of my ass cheeks.

I can feel all of it—but it isn't doing much for me.

I lean deeper into sensation.

I keep my eyes closed. I let Noah's hip thrusts choke me with his cock so that I gag. Bile wells up in my mouth and leaks out of the creases between my lips, mixing with the taste of latex.

"Oh yeah, baby," Noah's disembodied voice says. I don't know who in the room he's talking to.

Leah moans loudly again. She thrusts deeper into my cunt. I hear myself squeak around the dick stuffed deep in my face.

This still isn't doing much for me.

I lean deeper into my body's reactions.

I know my body. I know that if I gag over and over, at some point, my cunt will get wetter. I gag myself on Noah's cock. I hear Noah moan. I feel my body's involuntary reaction to gagging as my cunt gets wetter. I smell Leah's cunt and hear her come. I feel something thud onto the mattress beside Noah's thigh.

Leah pulls her dildo out of me.

She flops onto the mattress, on the other side of Broadsword's body.

I feel Noah anchoring both his hands into the mattress on either side of his hips so he can thrust into my face harder.

My eyes are watering. The pace of his thrusting is getting into the arena of inducing some mild breath play. Noah wants to come.

I shove latex and cock down my throat and let him. I feel his cock convulse through the static barrier of latex.

I keep my eyes closed as I open my mouth, raise myself up, and roll myself over Noah's thigh. I flop onto the bed between Noah and Leah.

"Sly, have you come?" Leah asks.

I keep my eyes closed and shake my head, no.

I feel Leah roll off the bed and hear a drawer open. I feel her climb back onto the bed and hold a vibrator against my cunt, just above my clit.

I feel her turn it on. I feel it buzz against me. I can smell latex and ejaculate and bodies as the vibrator relentlessly hums against my groin. I keep my eyes closed. I think about stardust, rope dust, and my favourite childhood playground, where I stood on the wooden edge of a sandbox, orating to the other children in gibberish, because before I even knew how to speak, I already knew I needed to be heard. I think about galaxies expanding and contracting and picture myself from outside myself, gagging on dick and involuntarily ejaculating while aliens in a playground build sandcastles around me.

I come, softly.

I feel water leaking out of my closed eyelids and running down my temples. I lose track of the form of my tears as they get lost in my hairline.

I find myself wondering who the fuck I am.

I keep my eyes closed for as long as is socially acceptable. I hope that when I open them, I'll be in a bubble, zooming through the cosmos, like a scene from *2001*, and that from that bubble, life will make sense to me.

I open my eyes.

Through the residual watery haze, I see that Leah and Noah are on either side of me again, looking down at me.

Leah gets up, takes off her black panty harness, and stands in front of the mirror, looking at her own naked body. I'm here, and I'm miles away. Noah picks up his phone off the bed—that must be what I felt thudding onto the bed next to us. I breathe.

It was a complicated sexual experience, but I'm okay. I'm depleted. Dopamine mingles with emotional exhaustion.

Tension I didn't realize I was carrying begins unravelling—from grinding to become an artist at night, from grinding at a job I'm miserable at during the day, from sleeping in too late each weekday, and from falling in and out of sleep every morning and every night while I commute on the subway.

James is leaving. I have no family who has earned the right to be called family. The vague sadness that's been weighing me down starts to take a concrete, expressible form. I'm sad because when James leaves, I'm not sure there will be anyone around who really knows me.

Leah's duvet is sweaty underneath me. Noah rolls onto his side to face Leah and me.

"So I went to take the photo you both agreed to, but I didn't realize my phone was in video mode. I ended up taking a video instead of a photo, accidentally. Don't worry, though, the two of you looked so sexy."

Every part of my body tenses back up immediately. Dealing with my sadness will have to wait.

"What?"

"Total accident. But you know, it's not easy to use a phone while getting a blow job," Noah says.

In my peripheral vision, Leah slumps to the floor in front of the mirror and says nothing.

Why isn't she saying anything?

This is her home. Her bedroom. Why isn't she saying anything?

Everything is so still that reality might be a TV show that's been paused.

Adrenalin kicks in.

I can feel my limbs get ready to fight, even as my soul pushes into my eyeballs.

Why is Noah behaving like this is cool and normal? Why isn't Leah looking at me?

I tell myself to behave calmly. There's two of them and one of me. I'm naked. There's a staircase between me and the apartment door. It would be hard for me to fight two people while running down a flight of stairs, if I make them angry. I tell myself to behave calmly until I know I can get away.

My mind starts cataloguing steps, like it's building a survival instruction manual. I can leave without finding my boxers. I need pants, shoes, and my jacket. Socks are too hard to get on. I don't need them. My pants are on the floor at the landing of the staircase. My jacket is hanging over the top of a barstool in the kitchen. My shoes are beside the front door. If I need to, I can just grab things, dress in the outer hallway, or bang on the neighbour's doors, like an assault victim in a movie of the week. They'll call the cops, and I'll have to talk to the Toronto Police Service about why I have sex with kinky strangers.

Why isn't Leah saying anything?

It's okay—if it comes to that, it comes to that. I'll look like a fool, I'll watch people shaking their heads, and I'll have to endure cops misgendering me. I'll be a cautionary story people tell about not letting unmet emotional needs outweigh rational judgment. Fuck it—if that's what it comes to, that's what it comes to. I need to see what's on the video so I can understand the extent to which I've been violated, and then I need to leave.

"Can I see the video?"

"Sure. I can send it to you too. All my media goes straight to the cloud, so it's easy to email transfer."

"Show me the video, please."

Leah stays lying on the floor in front of her mirror, staring silently at the ceiling.

Noah hands me his phone.

In little headspace, I'm hyperaware of the size of objects in relation to my size. Now, again, I feel this hyperawareness—but everything in the world has gotten exponentially bigger. Noah's phone is the size of a pizza box in my hands, and his hands are the size of car tires.

He reaches between my hands and presses play.

I see myself from outside of myself, without the benefit of my imagination, on the screen.

I see the events that took place while I was trying to reclaim an awkward social dynamic by leaning into physical sensation.

Onscreen, my eyes are closed as the video starts. I'm sucking Noah's dick.

Leah moans.

He pans up to her while she grinds her pelvis into my cunt.

The camera shakes as Noah tries to thrust into my face without the use of his arms because both of his hands are busy with camerawork.

I watch myself lean into his pelvis, watch myself gag, and watch spit leaking out of my mouth.

I hear him say, "Oh yeah, baby," as he films me gagging.

I hear Leah moan loudly from the phone speaker. He pans back up to her and my upturned ass.

I watch her thrust, deep and hard, into my cunt while looking straight into the camera.

Through the phone speaker, I hear myself squeak.

I watch the camera pan over to the mirror in the room so he can film all three of us and everything that is happening in the reflection.

I hear myself gag again and watch Leah come, plunging her dildo inside me, in the grainy image that Noah's cellphone is catching from the mirror's reflection.

He gives her a thumbs-up in the mirror.

The video playback ends.

It's too long a video, with too many pans and angles, to be an accident. The irony of Noah's patronizing tone regarding the cup of tea consent meme isn't lost on me in this moment.

At the same time, I'm way too terrified to explore ironies.

Noah asks me if I want to spend the night and offers to make up the couch for me to sleep on. I lie and say I have an early morning. I act as cool as I can. I make pleasant, flirty conversation whenever Noah seeks it to make sure that being filmed having sex without my knowledge and without my consent is the last traumatizing event that's going to occur this evening.

He walks me to the apartment door. He calls Leah to come say goodbye to me. She kisses me on the mouth without looking at me, like a little kid who has been instructed to show affection to a distant relation. Noah kisses me on the mouth too. I feel his faint stubble scrape against the edges of my lips.

I walk, in the late winter night, from Liberty Village to Toronto's east end, to my basement apartment. It takes me two hours. Time and space bend, and two hours pass like a lifetime, and like five minutes.

From the safety of distance, the next day, Daddy Broadsword and I have a text conversation.

I understand that yesterday you were okay with the video, and now your feelings have changed.

No, yesterday I was afraid for my life because you had just demonstrated how comfortable you are violating people. You never asked me if you could film me having sex with the two of you, so I never consented to it. Nothing about this was or will ever be okay.

I ask Broadsword not to contact or come near me again.

In response to my request to cease contact, he calls me.

I don't answer.

He leaves a voice mail. In the voice mail, he cries, alludes to terrible hardships he's experienced, and says he's still a work in progress.

I block Broadsword across all forms of contact and social media. Dagger, in turn, blocks me.

I hear from James that Broadsword decided to get the jump on narrating his version of the story by posting prolifically about our group sex on FetLife and spinning it.

Broadsword posts about how he still has a lot to learn about consent and is committed to becoming a more responsible dominant. He shares that he is honoured to do some serious soul-searching to improve himself through therapy. He shares that as part of a BDSM community that already endures societal stigma, he hopes his mistakes don't reflect poorly on the whole community.

My FetLife username gets thrown around in the online conversation through the course of Broadsword and Dagger pre-emptively calling themselves out so they can frame the conversion toward calling them back in.

I don't log on to FetLife for some time, on James's recommendation. When I do, I see rope scenesters I've met in passing and rope scenesters I've never even heard of posting their hot takes on my experience. Cis women rope bottoms clambering for any form of dialogue around dominance and consent applaud Broadsword for opening up about his need to improve, projecting their own hopes for a better kink scene onto his self-serving display of humility. I can't blame other rope bottoms for projecting their hopes for consensual, satisfying play onto Broadsword and Dagger— because that's what I was doing when I played with them.

Other cishet rope dudes dogpile on Broadsword's post, grateful for the opportunity to open up about their own struggles with mental health, self-control, and self-esteem. No one in the rope community who posts about my experience asks me if I'm okay. The rope community talks about me being videoed having sex without my knowledge or consent, but no one in the rope community wants to talk to me about it.

For anyone outside of the situation, it would look like a heart-warming upswell of rope community consciousness. I picture what it would be like to be someone else witnessing an online moment of group introspection, personal reckoning, and collective growth.

I imagine being someone else who walked into the warehouse BDSM party weeks earlier, wearing knock-off Louboutins, or second-hand workboots, or even a pair of soaking-wet sneakers, winterized by lining the inside with plastic grocery bags. I'd take any shoes other than my own.

I imagine being Vanessa instead of myself: the little who showed up, shared pencil crayons with a new friend, got a little spank, and went home safe, instead of staying to set up a date with a predator.

I wish I could be anyone else so I wouldn't have to know that Broadsword turned violating my consent into his own manipulative rebranding opportunity. Instead, I throw up in my mouth a little, and face facts while Broadsword and Dagger continue participating in the public rope scene together, continue being paid to perform, and continue working together, in person and online, to gain fetish subculture clout, cash, and credibility.

Alone together at the Shibari Salon, James asks me if he can hear Broadsword's voice mail. I haven't and won't be taking off my clothes. James and I are not having that kind of hangout. I bum a cigarette from him and light up while James holds my phone to his ear.

As he listens to Broadsword's sobbing, James says the only thing that makes me feel better, in my weeks of feeling angry, trapped, scared, gaslit, and voiceless.

"What crocodile tears. Sly, don't believe anything Broadsword says, ever."

"I don't believe him."

"Good."

For a long time after being filmed without my consent, I think about the limits to which I can trust what I want.

I think about Broadsword bringing up how all people in fetish face stigma just so he could draw empathy from the margins by invoking a shared sense of marginalization.

When a subculture is built around the idea of being shunned and shamed by mainstream society, popular figures in that community become synonymous with the subculture itself. It makes it hard to critique and call out abusive behaviour because it can be seen as a betrayal or an attack on the subculture as a whole. In this way, a lot of the time, it's easier for BDSM communities to tolerate gaslighting, consent breaches, and harm. While all these negatively impact individuals, ignoring those impacts maintains the existence, unity, and, at least on a surface level, the cohesion of the larger kink community. I think about the moments in the kink scene when I've been complicit in these dynamics. I had worried about the two women leashed by the creepy guy who owned the BDSM studio but said nothing so I could continue seeking out the rope fix I wanted.

I unpack every motivation I had, from desire, to sadness, to grief. I replay every moment of every interaction I had with Broadsword and Dagger to map out every time I should have walked away.

I think about the space I crave to be raw, volatile, wild, and free through fetish—and I wonder if that means I'll always be vulnerable to my cravings being co-opted.

I'm not a community or a person invested in making a scene happen—I'm just rolling solo through life and trying to figure out who I am. I realize that even if I'm going to keep searching for myself through kink with strangers in shitty warehouse parties run by creepy misogynists and their hangers-on, and my filters for sussing out harmful actors aren't filtering out enough, that still doesn't make me responsible for other people's predatory behaviour. But it does mean I need to ask myself hard questions. While it's good to be reminded that I can survive, I need to ask myself how much capacity I have to repeat the act of surviving over and over before I start losing more than I'm gaining along the way.

I take a break from the Toronto rope community and slip into rope bondage obscurity immediately. Bottoms come and go from the cishet rope scene, like a conveyor belt, and no one notices or asks questions. I give up the ongoing emotional relationship I have with rope bondage and the freedom it gives me. If I come across good people who happen to tie, I'll engage in bondage again, but I do not go looking for new riggers anymore.

I bid adieu to my love affair with dealers of jute. I lose access to a feral, unfettered, sensual part of myself in the process.

For those of us with ugly personal histories that we didn't choose but have to learn to live with, BDSM and playing with the perception of danger can be healing—like a form of low-budget, DIY exposure therapy—but the perception of danger is more therapeutic that the real threat of it is.

I slowly recognize that I've been without the support frameworks I need for so long that I'm too used to manifesting therapeutic dynamics in whatever circumstances I find myself in—whether those therapeutic dynamic are really on offer or just an act of my wilful imagination.

Sex can be healing, and kink is a place of self-discovery, but if I expect sex clubs and dungeons to completely heal my trauma, to hold space for my gender identity, and to satisfy my need for family, then I'm likely to get burned as often as I get what I'm looking for.

I start looking to surround myself with more like-minded people, knowing I might not find them and that my loneliness may get worse before it gets better.

I start trying to live more in the real dynamics present around me—in kink, in sex, and in life—and start trying to live in my imagination less.

BEING A BOTTOM

My fingers run across the latte-coloured, felt-lined interior of a twenty-year-old Volkswagen Golf, as the frame of the car rattles from the speed we're driving at. We blow past a controlled burn that's consuming palm trees in flames along the side of the road while blasting Robyn from a CD we picked up at a suburban outlet mall. We're on Stuart Highway, which is an arterial road that cuts across the continent of Australia, top to bottom. Despite being a major highway, it often whittles down to a two-lane stretch of asphalt in the middle of nowhere. The driving hazards on Stuart Highway include criminals hiding from the law in the outback, all cellphone and radio service cutting out, and kangaroos bounding onto the road in front of you.

Kyle's in the driver's seat beside me, on the opposite side of the car than I'd expect. Driving is on the left side of the road here instead of the right. Ever since we got to Australia, I keep walking to the wrong side of the car and looking the wrong way before I cross the street, instinctively out of sync with the world around me.

We're living and working in seaside cities along the northern Australian coast, often closer to Timor-Leste than to any of the Australian capitals where one might find a Real Housewives franchise. Coming from my hometown of Montreal and having lived in dense population centres like Toronto and Vancouver, being in regional Australia feels like I'm on the edge of the map, in the uncharted unknown where a medieval cartographer would have just drawn a dragon. Addiction is a debilitating problem in the towns here, as are violence and property crime. One of the region's main industries, mining, is a straight-up unsafe sector for anyone who is AFAB to work in because of gendered sexual harassment and gendered sexual violence in the workplace. While this fact makes headlines in Sydney and Melbourne, in northern Australia, where the problem is prominent, it is only whispered about at bars after three rounds of drinks as women confess why they're really leaving their careers in favour of moving back in with their parents.

Kyle and I run into a surprising number of people missing part of a limb as we go about our lives in this place that is new to us. People who live here tend to go swimming in the landscape's fresh and salt waterways, but no waterway in Australia's north is guaranteed to be crocodile-free. Luxury brands own crocodile farms here so they can turn croc skins into handbags worth six figures. Only intrepid reporters talk about this because the luxury brands source skins here under ambiguous subsidiaries. When I arrive and look through the job classifieds, there are vacancies open for crocodile-egg collectors, who will be helicoptered to wild nests and lowered on rope ladders from the sky to gingerly steal unhatched crocodile eggs, giving alarming accuracy to the statement, "Here be dragons."

The cities and towns in Australia's north exist largely to extract naturally occurring resources from the land, to extract athletes and artists from rural communities, to make money off tourism, and to serve joint Australian-American military interests. It's an area at the nexus of many tensions, and the area operates with minimal genuine oversight. Civil servants with lifetime job security funnel government money to their friends with impunity, wear flip-flops in the office, and complain about how much better things used to be, despite the fact that they earn salaries upward of $200K annually.

Within this context, there are also many kind, well-intentioned workers who try to amplify the environmental and cultural experiences that make the region amazing so that the towns are more equitable and enjoyable places to live. Unfortunately, the ratio of kind, cool people who also get burnt out is high, as they face the full scope of the colonial, corporate, and corrupt forces they're up against. While a lot of people push for social justice, others grip tightly to exploiting the region and its social problems for personal gain. The retail spaces, office buildings, and apartments here are only fractionally occupied. A large mining project closed a few years earlier, causing a huge exodus of workers and their families. Without jobs, upward of ten thousand people had no other reason to stay. Now, the central business districts of so many of these cities are ghost towns struggling to define their futures.

The collision of the realities evident here crosses my mind constantly: the wildness of the outback, the natural beauty of the coast, the cruel banality of small-town cronyism, and the local impacts of international interests and globalization. These realities exist everywhere, but in bigger cities, they're not as transparent.

I scroll Instagram, where celebs show off their crocodile-leather Birkins. I drive by military bases. I eat croc burgers in neighbourhood pubs—a meat that's cheaper than beef here because of all the flesh under those valuable skins. I overhear patronizing CEOs talking themselves up to anyone who will listen while they allot themselves three-hour lunch breaks in the middle of the work-day. I watch curlews fly, land, and bow to each other, displaying a natural sense of manners and majesty. I look out at the most stunning tropical sunsets I have ever seen.

I know that part of the dissonance I feel is a matter of my own culture shock, but acknowledging that does nothing to help me shake off the dissonance. This place takes a bite out of people—figuratively, in terms of normalizing injustice, and literally, in terms of croc attacks. I've spent years of my life escaping into my imagination as a survival mechanism, but I couldn't manifest the surreal facts and fantasies of northern Australia in my mind's eye even if I tried. I don't want to use my imagination to make my reality more tolerable anymore, so while here, I live in what's real and at the edge of my capacity to keep it together.

Kyle and I arrived in Australia through a shared will to run away from everything we've ever known, not really sure what we're running toward, but very sure that we're ready to move past where we've been.

Kyle and I have been dating for a year with a lot of consistency, but a lot of fluctuation and change in our lives otherwise. I take a part-time job running an arts company in Calgary, which eats up my psychic space full-time and requires overtime from me in the form of unpaid emotional labour. Kyle and I have a long-distance-short-distance relationship and trade off taking the one-hour flight between Calgary and Vancouver to see each other. It makes every one of our dates feel like a special occasion.

Back in Vancity, Kyle begins using they and them pronouns.

Having been their lover and partner for a while, I'm not surprised. When I met them on Tinder, their profile read like an open-minded, 420-friendly bi guy, but the curated carousel of pictures in their profile screamed, "I'm in egg mode!"

It's an honour and a privilege to watch Kyle come out about being trans in their own ways, in their own time, and on their own terms.

They aren't experiencing a personal revelation—they've known they aren't cisgender for a very long time. The claiming of new pronouns is a means for them to name that to the world and to renegotiate their relationship with society on more accurate terms.

Their new pronouns, and the way they ever so slightly change their gender presentation at work, have an immediate negative impact on the way they are treated. It's a hard pill to swallow in a major Canadian city in the 2010s after being in their job their whole adult life. The friend squad they roll with doesn't roll with the news particularly well, either. A bunch of Kyle's friends begin confiding in them, as if Kyle's gender identity is a troubling secret, so now it must be Kyle's responsibility to hold the squad's troubling secrets too. Their relationships with their friends become an icky mess of trauma bonds unravelling. Kyle moves through a difficult time of reconciling the fact that they were born and raised in Vancouver, with a lifetime of connections to the place, with the fact that the reason they never came out about being trans before now was because a lifetime of connections didn't equate to having real allies who would offer real support without wanting something in return.

In high school, Kyle's friend group was different. Back then, Kyle and their friends were shaggy-haired, emo pop-punk Soulcalibur aficionados. Every one of Kyle's friends was either a closeted queer or a trans kid in egg mode—but they all went to a Catholic high school, so none of them ever talked about it. Even so, they all shared a sense of being aliens on the down-low. That was what drew them to being friends. In their group, everyone normalized teen boys playing video games as women characters, even if they never articulated why it felt normal. High school graduation rolled around, and some of Kyle's friends went on to live more openly queer lives, some fell into ketamine addiction, and some directly started entry-level work in industries. Some, like Kyle, got pressured to be successful in a traditionally capitalistic, cishet sense: use the means at your family's disposal to study for a well-paying career, date a nice cishet girl you meet at your university, get a job in the well-paying career you studied for, and then marry that cishet girl and start saving for the next generation's education. It's a life afforded of class privilege, and a life a lot of people would want. It's also a life where the trajectory of everything is decided at the age of eighteen, with little margin for error, change, or transition.

Kyle choked on that trajectory even as they wove their way through it during university. Every time they crew-cut their hair, they were told how handsome and successful they looked. Every time they put on a suit instead of a dress, they were told they looked hirable and desirable. They constantly received approval and praise for adhering to AMAB gender norms. They constantly got told how lucky they were to have cis male privilege, quietly enduring the gaslighting of being told to appreciate the ease of being a man when they weren't a man at all. At Vancouver lesbian events, they were shunned. At Vancouver gay events, they were objectified and treated like twink fresh meat. At Vancouver straight events, they were expected to pick up the tab. In class, they were told to take the lead. In their sex life, they were told to follow the lead—being AMAB, it's enforced to you over and over that you must want all the sex you are offered, at all times. Frameworks of gender diversity and spectrums of sexuality that include asexuality didn't exist in a widely acknowledged way yet. Through this early adulthood, they received positive reinforcement to drink to manage anxiety, to have random sex to establish self-worth, and to be anyone other than the trans feminine person that they were so that they would be well-liked, respected, and prosperous.

Kyle lived with near-constant unease the deeper they got into their educational and societal training at university. The closer they got to the graduation finish line, the more they feared that all the time and energy they'd put into their education would be for nothing. They feared losing the financial mobility a career would give them if they came out about being trans. They feared that all they'd be left with was a story to whisper at bars, after three rounds of drinks, about why they gave up on success in favour of moving back in with their parents.

As Kyle starts using they and them pronouns, I watch the pain they're in diminish their capacity for compassion. They become more rigid in their stances. They snap at people. They grab the wheel of conversations and swerve the conversations back to talking about themself. Kyle has been what other people want them to be for so long that they don't have enough of themself left to offer to anybody any generosity.

At night, when they intermittently rustle awake, they pull me close, kiss the back of my neck, and say, "I love you so fucking much, Sly."

The rest of the time, during the waking world, they're a raw nerve.

As Kyle's employer gets passive-aggressive about their change in gender presentation, Kyle starts hearing from colleagues down under who are eager to recruit structural engineers from overseas. Especially in regional and rural areas, the shortage of skilled workers is downright critical. Kyle can't afford to quit their job in Vancouver and still make Yaletown rent, so they move into my place in Alberta while they figure out what's next. We live together for the first time. By the time they get a job offer from Australia, the conversation in our relationship has transformed from "Should you do this?" to "Should we do this?"

It's too early for our relationship to take this leap of faith across the world, but we're a trans-4-trans couple. It's hard for us to make choices that would isolate us from each other when we already feel so isolated from society. So we sell most of what we own and fly across the world. It's an act of desperation, bravery, commitment, and self-preservation, on both of our parts, in different ways.

I look out the window of our twenty-year-old Volkswagen. We zoom past abandoned storefronts that used to be lively outdoor malls and arcades in coastal boom times. We look out the window in fear as we drive past gum trees on fire. Embers and charred palm fronds dance on the wind. I mouth along to the track "Send to Robin Immediately" blaring from the dash, as Robyn sings about having nothing to lose as long as you've got someone to love.

We pull up to Sexyland along Stuart Highway.

Sexyland is a chain of sex toy department stores that takes a big box, fast food approach to intimacy. Their online store boasts twenty-four-hour delivery direct from their warehouses, seven days a week, within two hours of placing an order. At all moments in Australia, whether you're dreaming or doom-scrolling, somewhere the staff in a sex toy warehouse are picking and packing vibrators, furry handcuffs, Fleshlights, and lube. I always imagine it to be like the final scene of the first Indiana Jones movie, except that instead of stowing away the Ark of the Covenant, they're fetching a big spender the Pipedream Extreme Fuck Me Silly Mega Masturbator. People need and deserve so much pleasure as means of decompression and resilience—especially here, in the middle of nowhere. The chain doesn't end up in tourism ads for Australia, but Sexyland is as emblematic of Australia as the koala. Their outlet stores are vast and ugly, passing on savings to their customers by spending absolutely no money on decor. This particular Sexyland is part of an outdoor strip mall facing the road, with windows of mannequins wearing ill-fitting maid costumes. If the mannequins aren't enticing enough, outside there are signs with big red bubble letters that read, "Huge Range" and "Fantasies!"

My relationship with Kyle is the first in which I'm consistently someone's top in a kinky capacity. It's not a role that fits me, but I've been topped enough that I've learned how to do it well through osmosis. In playing with and dominating Kyle, I act like the best parts of Evie; I bring an imitation of her dominance, intuition, and curiosity to how I top Kyle.

It's a pattern I fall into without meaning to. When I'd visit Kyle in their Yaletown apartment, they'd be craving an escape from anxiety, even though they had fridge full of beer and a cupboard full of luxury cannabis crossbreeds. They were in the market for a dominant. For me, being a bottom helped me find clarity when I needed it, so I get it. I didn't know any responsible Vancity dominants I could recommend, and I was a bit curious about what being a dom might show me about myself. So, I fell into the practice of dominating them and providing that kind of escape.

As Kyle fell asleep next to me in their Yaletown home, they would tell me that they were such a greedy, sexy sub, they brought out the dom in everyone. I'd tell them to go to sleep and lie next to them, wide awake, my brain racing.

I didn't want to disrupt any narrative in which they found pride or grounding, especially not when they were emotionally vulnerable. At the same time, Kyle was not so compelling a bottom that they transformed me into someone who got off on being dominant—because no one could be. The first few times I tied Kyle up, clipped clothespins to their nipples, then painfully flicked them off, I can't say it wasn't interesting, because it was. It's always a rush to step into a new role for the first time and to realize an untapped ability. It made me feel strong. But the rush of the novelty of playing dom wore thin, and my relationship with Kyle didn't rewrite my DNA around intimacy.

In my sleeplessness, I let my mind wander where it needed to. I might be emotionally supporting Kyle, but I was still catching up on processing my own life's events too.

Evie and I meet outside of Ashes Concert Hall in Toronto on a chilly Halloween night. The headlights driving up and down Sherbourne Street blur in the backgrounds of photos as partygoers grab selfies of their outfits before they head in. Tonight's event at Ashes is an annual kink and play party run by a latex and leather goods brand. Once you get past the bouncers, the event has a strict no-photo policy due to all the nudity.

Evie's wearing her once-a-year makeup and tells me to kiss her neck instead of her face. Her clumpy dark-burgundy lipstick is matte and reminds me of a black hole, absorbing light and swallowing worlds. She's dressed to play in a black bodysuit and thigh-high black stiletto boots, with a teeny tiny backpack slung over her shoulder. Only certain kinds of sex toys could be stowed away in a bag that small. My head swirls with the possibilities.

"One of the things I love about playing with you is that we never plan our scenes. They just flow intuitively."

"That's all you. You're amazing."

"No Sly, that's us together," Evie answers. I'm mostly naked under my coat. I couldn't afford to buy a look, so I'm wearing black briefs and flat-soled black-leather boots, stained and cracked from many years of dance floors. I give Evie a peek under my coat.

"Your body is the accessory."

"My body is yours," I answer.

I kiss her neck, she grabs my hand, and we head into the party.

Every hallway, bathroom, and cavernous space inside Ashes is windowless, black-walled, and full of people. There are easily over a thousand people here. Next to Burning Man or a sex expo in Las Vegas, this is probably the most kinksters any of us will ever see at one time, in one place—and it feels great. Bears and otters tend to clump together, and there are corners of the space that feel more heterosexual than others, but at the meeting points between demographics, magic happens. Compliments are given and received across the boundaries of sexual orientation, and fandom is expressed for the way scenes play out, regardless of the genders involved. There's a lot of mutual respect and appreciation thrown around between otherwise separate kink communities.

Fetish has the power to break down the importance of sexual orientation and gender, because fetish takes sex and sensuality out of the realm of which genitals are touching which genitals and into the realm of fuller body experiences, where the soft back of a knee or the hard palate at the top of a wide-open mouth are more intense centres of pleasure than cocks and clits. In this way, fetish can render gender and sexual orientation to be irrelevant, when it comes to sensory experience. Broader social hang-ups still impact who attends which fetish events—usually. This party at Ashes is one of the few kink events that manages to make fetish as socially subversive and as societally healing as it has the potential to be, through sheer scale and size. If you're kinky in Toronto, you're here.

Evie and I pass the straight guy who runs the Black Mask Bondage Extravaganza. We only recognize him because he's wearing a custom leather jacket with "Black Mask" stitched across the back of it. In the straight rope scene, Black Mask is a big deal, but here at Ashes, he's just one of the rest of us. Evie isn't impressed with his flex.

"You know you're important when you have to wear a jacket with your own name on it," she laughs.

We wind our way through the hallways to the biggest chamber, which is usually a concert stage and a mosh pit. Tonight, the space has been transformed, with kink performance stages and open play spaces that are free for anyone to use but organized, roped off, and maintained by a team of dungeon monitors.

Dungeon monitors are basically bouncers for kink, and their job is to make sure that any play taking place is safe, sane, and consensual. They stay within eyeshot and earshot of all the scenes. If a person calls "red" during play but the dominant doesn't listen, a dungeon monitor will step in and end the scene. If a DM feels that a person is not in fit state to give consent— if they look upset, inebriated, or like they're being coerced—a DM won't let the scene happen. Anyone who refuses to obey a dungeon monitor will be immediately ejected. Dungeon monitors are usually dominants or switches themselves and able to tell the difference between consensual play, even if it gets intense, and abusive behaviour.

Evie and I stop to watch two gay leather daddies engage in an inner-thigh-spanking scene in one of the roped off play areas. I'm standing with my bisexual, cisgender dom, amidst a crowd that doesn't care what anyone's sexual orientation or gender is. We're all just living sensory receptors, huddling in the dark, watching consensual pleasure and pain, while we try to figure out what to do with the gift and burden of consciousness. Everything, both beautiful and troubling, is out in the open.

"This is the world I want to live in," I tell Evie.

The risks associated with public and private play are different—especially at an event this big. When you're playing at a public event, you can't control who might watch your scene, and you have to trust that people will respect the photo ban. At the same time, when playing in private there's no DM to call out to, or anyone to back up your version of events, after the fact. There's a level of control given up and gained, in both circumstances. I love playing in public, because I love dungeon monitors. It'd be great if I could have a DM around all the time, watching, checking in, and reminding me that I don't have to make choices that don't serve me.

At the centre of the roped-off play area, a few feet away from the gay leather daddies, there's an apparatus no one's claimed. It's a lime-green dome made out of steel—a jungle gym, like you'd find on a playground. Surrounded by other torture equipment, it looks out of place, like a mirage. Evie likes standing out in a crowd and likes mind-fucking the people witnessing our play. Tonight's no exception.

"The dome?" she asks.

"Absolutely," I answer.

Evie gets permission from one of the DMs to enter the roped-off area and use the unclaimed equipment. I get down on my hands and knees to crawl inside the dome through one of the gaps between bars, while Evie steps through a gap in the bars higher up, like a sexy spy in a summer blockbuster. She crouches down in her high-heeled boots and opens up her tiny backpack. She pulls out a few reams of rope, a blunt little spanking paddle, and a pair of safety shears, good for sliding between rope and skin. The last thing she pulls out is a roll of shiny black duct tape.

I back up into the structure of the dome gently and rub my spine and ass against the cold steel. The living sensory receptor that I am loves being restrained and constrained. At many points, my life has been such a structureless, irrational mess. I crave structure so deeply; I prefer if it's a thing I can feel and see around me. Within structure, I feel safe enough to be free.

Evie steps toward me with rope. I'm excited. She ties my torso into the steel dome so that my arms and legs are free, but at the same time, I'm not going anywhere.

The dungeon monitor who let us into the play space walks by. He's staying a respectful distance from our scene so we don't feel intruded on, but he's also making sure to do his job. He makes eye contact with me and holds my gaze long enough to let me know that he's there. He's an older cis guy, on the shorter side and dressed all in black, with frizzy grey hair. His eye contact lets me know that he's here for me, if I need him. I feel the security he offers me from across the room, even though we've never spoken or exchanged names.

Evie picks up the blunt paddle but doesn't use it right away. She builds slowly, first warming up the skin she's going to whale on by rubbing it with an open palm so that I'm drawn into sensation, rather than shocked by it. She steps up from rubbing to slapping my skin with her palm and then applies the paddle to my ass cheeks. The paddle's a harsh motherfucker, despite its small size, and I scream into the busy, cacophonous room. Out of the corner of my eye, I can see Evie flourishing in having an audience, enjoying the strength and agility of her own body just as much as she's getting off on making me scream. The DM makes eye contact with me again—unobtrusive but present. I give him a smile and a nod, and he nods back. We've got a wordless dialogue going.

Evie weaves in and out of the dome, stepping through the holes between bars and whaling on my chest, ass, and thighs with her paddle. My skin feels hot and raw from her paddling but cold and covered in goosebumps from the steel I'm tied into. She stands close to my face and looks into my eyes. She kisses me, then pulls away. She's made a mess of her makeup by kissing me, but her eyes remain calm and pleased.

She crouches down and picks up the roll of black duct tape. She and I have never played with duct tape before, and I've never had duct tape put on me. She yanks a foot of the tape off the roll and holds the outstretched tape in front of my mouth. Our consent code: she shows me what she has in mind, and I can shake my head no, or nod my head yes. If I nod, this will be the most intense session of bottoming I have ever done, tied into steel and walloped in public, with industrial-strength tape gagging me. Time and space fold, and a moment lasts a lifetime. I contemplate whether I can take being a bottom this far and whether I want to go this deep.

I make eye contact with the DM. He's watching.

I feel emboldened.

I look at Evie, at the tape outstretched in front of me, and nod my head. Yes.

She plasters the duct tape over my mouth and wraps the roll around my head so the tape is across my cheeks, around the base of my neck, and in my hair. I realize that being wrapped in the duct tape is one thing—being pulled out of it will be another.

I breathe through my nose, deeply, and close my eyes, feeling the tape's strength and tightness. I breathe into the structure and constraints. As a bottom, I've played a lot of ways and done a lot of things. This is different. Duct tape is different.

"Stomp a foot on the floor if you need out, want to stop, or need to check in," Evie tells me.

I open my eyes, look up at her, and nod again.

She steps away from me, and I see the DM wanting to catch my eye, knowing that now I can't speak. He's waiting for me to reconfirm, without words, that I'm where I want to be. I give him a nod. He nods back at me.

Evie builds slowly again, rubbing my skin that is both brutalized red and icy cold. She slaps lightly at first, then faster, then faster and harder, and I let out a stifled scream.

I scream into the tape and feel what it means to have access to only one airway instead of two. I learn the inner world of this intense form of bondage. Because I can't suck air into my lungs quickly through my mouth, I need to keep a level of steadiness to my breathing. The fact that I need to keep my breath steady means that this is not a scene where I can get raw and ragged in the ways I'm used to. This scene will need my composure. I won't get to lose myself in the moment or become animalistic.

Evie steps through to the outside of the dome and wallops my ass with the paddle. I scream again and catch myself.

I bring myself back to my breath. In and out, through my nose. Steady.

She wallops me again. I can see the DM watching. I feel the intense pain, but I focus on breathing and react less—so I feel the sensations more.

I feel the smart and sting of the paddle against my ass. I feel my sphincter contract, and I feel the chain reaction of the sensations running down my legs, tingling from the tips of my toes to the edges of my teeth. I feel sensation climbing up my spine, filling the negative space at the back of my neck and making me hyperaware of the tape gunk squishing into my buzz-cut hair.

Evie climbs up the outside of the jungle gym—I can't see her, but I can feel her crawling up the outside of the structure behind me.

She gently nuzzles the toe of her boot into the cotton of my briefs to nudge my ass cheeks apart.

Through the cotton of my underwear, my asshole contracts over and over against the toe of her foot.

I picture what she must look like, hanging off the outside of the dome, one hand holding onto a bar, one foot anchored on another bar, one hand holding the paddle, and one foot gingerly buried in my brutalized butt, while I stand there underneath her, bound, gagged, and wide eyed.

Evie likes to put on a show. She's as fascinating and inscrutable as the night sky, and she needs people to know it.

She whales on my ass again and on the back of my thighs with her paddle.

I feel the pain of all of it, breathing in through my nose, out through my nose, and telling myself to keep steady. The pain feels all the more extra for my inability to yell out about it. I feel the skin on my ass getting rougher and rawer. I feel abrasions swelling up, changing the landscape of my skin.

I feel a stiletto heel in my back, placed firmly, but with control and restraint, against one of my shoulder blades.

I feel an equally controlled and restrained pressure from Evie as she presses the sole of one of her boots into the back of my head.

Ever so slightly, she uses her toe to bow my head forward.

The steel dome creates a context in which it feels like the laws of nature do not apply. I can be standing up, and Evie can walk all over me. Gravity doesn't exist.

She climbs down from the outside of the dome, slips her body through the bars again, and stands in front of me. She slaps my chest while looking into my eyes.

Sounds squirm out of my mouth and get stuck to my lips, held in place by tape gunk.

She kisses me again, on top of the tape gagging my mouth, so I can feel the pressure of her mouth but can't feel any detail.

It's a kiss that's blunt and imprecise. It's a kiss that isn't a kiss. It sends endorphins rushing through me. Her face, pressing into mine through bondage, sends me even deeper in subspace.

A thousand suns go supernova around us. Evie's an alien too, made of fire and light. My cunt contracts. My cock swells. I want to come everywhere.

She walks over to her tiny backpack and bends over slowly, to put on a show. She's sculpted her ass with daily mixed martial arts training, and she loves it. She puts her nasty little paddle back in her teeny tiny backpack.

She walks back to me and climbs up the inside of the cage this time, using her sculpted strength to hold herself up on the inside of the cage with just her arms. In this pull-up, she rests one of her stiletto heels on my chest and rests the other boot's toe against my mouth, pressing slightly and with a lot of control into the duct tape.

A kiss that isn't a kiss, and every one of Evie's limbs an instrument of ecstasy.

I look up at her and shudder with sheer delight at her power, at how good her leather boot feels on my gagged mouth, at the degree of strength and control it takes for her to be holding herself up above me.

Her boot on my mouth, on top of the duct tape, makes it feel like there's dominance on top of dominance happening, and like I'm bottoming from within bottoming. I'm so deep in subspace that an undiscovered asteroid belt just whisked by us, scraping my ass cheeks and bruising my tits.

It might take a lifetime for me to come back to planet Earth, if I ever bother coming back at all.

I don't remember anything about my existence before this moment. All I know is that Evie's doing a gravity-defying ballet on my mouth, that I can feel her weight pushing into my upturned face, and that this is the most spectacular moment I have ever experienced.

If I could speak, I would tell her that I will never again see anything as otherworldly.

She climbs down the inside of the dome, scuttling her body over mine. I catch the DM's eyes again—he's been watching the whole time, ready to catch whatever my eyes have to say.

Evie unties the rope binding me to the cage. She holds my torso as she guides me to where I need to be, slumped on the floor.

Subspace begins to blend with reality. The black void of the cosmos begins to shift into the black walls of Ashes. Evie lets me rest a moment. The scene isn't over. The most intense sensation of all is yet to come.

Her fingernails loosen the edge of the duct tape at the back of my head. She kisses me through the tape again, one last time, and looks me in the eye.

"This is really going to hurt. Are you ready?"

I look up at her through a beaded curtain of stars, and I can see the dungeon monitor standing and watching from behind Evie.

I nod my head. Yes.

Evie rips the duct tape off from around my head in one swift, sharp, extremely painful movement.

I scream as I feel the duct tape rip out my hair.

I burst into tears.

Evie scoops me up in her arms, carries me to a sofa, and holds me in her lap while I cry.

The shock of the tape ripping out my hair brings on an intense realization. I don't express it in words. Instead I sit in Evie's lap, bawling. The crystal-clear realization that pushes through all the sensations still reverberating through me, through all the screams and squeals from other ongoing BDSM scenes, and through the endless rotation of nearby planetary systems, is not what I expected to find through the deepest and ugliest bit of bottoming I've ever done.

I sit there crying, knowing with absolute certainty that I'm done being a bottom.

I would change nothing about our scene, or about any of the consensual fetish I've engaged in. As I sit in Evie's lap, I don't feel remorse or regret. Instead, through the folds of space and time, I feel my journey of being a bottom coming to an end.

That was my last scene.

I don't need to hurt anymore.

I open the car door and step onto sizzling-hot asphalt while Kyle walks around the car to join me. They take my hand, and we walk toward Sexyland.

The door chimes to announce customers as Kyle holds it open for me. A bored Millennial looks up at us from behind the cash desk at the centre of store. She's got long, dark hair with a strip of hot pink dyed into it, as though emo pop-punk never went out of style—or maybe here, those sensibilities have only just arrived. She tells us to let her know if we need help finding what we're looking for.

For a moment, I want to tell this rural retail employee that I don't know who I am anymore, and that's what I'm here in Australia, in a sex toy department store off a highway, to look for.

Kyle and I walk around, taking in all of Sexyland's offerings. The bored Millennials who work here don't seem to care about cleaning, and most of the stock is covered with a faint film of dust and despair. There's an impulse-buy bin of easy-to-install under-mattress ankle and wrist restraints. There are *Fifty Shades of Grey*–branded satin ties and blindfolds. There's a line of lubes called Shibari—snagging a word for rope bondage and co-opting it to make lubricant seem new, edgy, and on trend. I want so badly to be turned on by any of the toys Kyle and I walk by, but my dick is limp as fuck about everything.

At the back of the store, there's a wall-mounted flip rack of different porn film covers, with discs behind the counter available for purchase. The year is 2019, but buying hard copies of porn is still a relevant practice here, off Stuart Highway. There are a ton of rural areas that don't have internet access. I realize that my whole adult life, I've taken access to PornHub for granted. Kyle slides up beside me, and we share stories about masturbation fantasies, as prompted by the porn titles—*Co-Pilots Cum Harder*, *Gay Frats Boys Fuck Faster*, and the almost romantic-sounding incest fantasy film, *Brother, Watch Me While I Watch You*. Another couple comes into the store in a rush: she's ass out, wearing a bikini, and he isn't wearing shoes. This far north in Australia, retailers cannot enforce "No Shirt, No Shoes, No Service." Kyle and I vent about our shared culture shock in rural Australia. My jadedness and judgment of the whole northern Australian vibe is my way of covering for how out of place I feel, as I try to re-author with intentionality my relationship with sex and sensuality, as drunk white guys walk by me in bare feet, and as I'm surrounded by a catalogue of outdated, meth-fuelled pornography.

A few months after our public play at Ashes, I travel back to Toronto for work. Evie and I haven't talked much, but she's sent me a few text updates. She's living with Michael, her investment banker boyfriend. She's bought the beagle puppy. She and Michael have been workshopping what to tell his parents about what she does for a living. Neither of them thinks honesty is an option. Evie's been reshaping her life every day because she's been losing business at an alarming rate; regular clients she's had for a long time have been dropping her services. It's drastically impacting her monthly income as someone who is a self-employed freelancer. I text her back and offer updates of my own that are bland and supportive. She's going through it, so I try not to complain too much about how my own self-employed artist hustle is failing and flailing.

I haven't figured out how to tell Evie that my heart isn't in bottoming anymore. She is amazing, and I know that if we don't have a dom/sub dynamic, there's little overlap left between our existences.

Instead of meeting up to play and fuck, we decide to drive to a hiking trail she's found through some listicle so we can walk her new dog and go on a different kind of adventure.

Evie pulls up to our meeting place in a minivan. She's borrowed it from one of Michael's cousins, she explains, as she rolls the window down to surprise me. She's dressed like a soccer mom, in a puffer vest and sweatpants that have seen better days. She's got the beagle in the back seat. It's bizarre to see the globe-trotting pro dom I've known for years transformed into a vision of suburban realness—although maybe most globe-trotting pro doms drive their dogs around in minivans in their off-hours. I know lots of kinksters who have very normcore lives outside of fetish—I've just never seen the normcore side of Evie.

Even though she's driving, she can't put down her phone. FOSTA and SESTA bills have just been signed into law in the United States. Evie's in a state of complex, complete, and well-justified panic. These new laws are having an immediate and devastating impact on all sex workers and pro doms who use the internet to advertise their services—which is pretty much all sex workers and pro dominants. Between GPS driving instructions and barks from the peppy puppy in the back seat, I watch Evie chug Starbucks and move through a meltdown.

We talk about the fact that Backpage.com has been seized and is no longer in operation. The personal ads on Craigslist have disappeared. We talk about how this internet crackdown, which is supposed to prevent sex trafficking, will just make it harder for everyone in the consensual sex work industry to screen clients for safety, ironically making professional sex workers more vulnerable to non-consensual sex trafficking and to violence from clients. FOSTA-SESTA is bad in general, but because of her dwindling regular client roster, for Evie it's really the worst news with the worst timing.

"Do you know anything about backing up websites from when you did IT? I don't want to have to rebuild my website from scratch if it gets taken down."

"Do you have all the text and image files that appear on your website stored anywhere other than your website? So that at least you'll have all the content in some form, even if it's not organized?"

"No, I built my business website over time. Maybe I've got some photos on my laptop, and some on my phone ..."

"I'd recommend logging in to the back end of your website and seeing if you can download all the images you've uploaded. If there's no better mechanism available, I suggest you copy and paste all the text you've written on your website into a Word file. Just so you don't have to recreate everything if your website is deleted by whatever service you use to host it."

"What if my website gets deleted today? Do you think I should just screenshot my whole website so that I have something?"

"It won't give you images with a good enough resolution that you'll want to reuse them, but yes, screenshotting every page of your website would be good. That way you'll have a record of the content, the layout, and everything you've put thought and time into."

"Do you think I should pull over and screenshot my website now?"

"Absolutely, if you want to. Whatever you need."

We pull over. I pet Evie's new dog while she screengrabs everything she's got online. She takes a deep breath when she's done, turns on the ignition, and drives the minivan back onto the road. We both watch the windshield wipers whip back and forth. She asks me to start a conversation, but all I can think about how rough things are financially, for her, for me, and for almost every queer and trans person I know. I search my mind for something uplifting to say without sounding trite. I come up with nothing.

It's a drizzly spring day in Ontario. Evie leashes the puppy, and I feel a genuine pang of jealousy for a moment. I don't want to be leashed by Evie again, but I remember what it was like to be her puppy—and I can feel that if I'm not her puppy, we don't really connect anymore.

"I'm kind of jealous of your dog, and I'm having a hard time grappling with that feeling."

"I can walk you on a leash again."

"I don't think it's that kind of jealousy. This little pup has found a great owner—you—and now throughout her life, this is it. She can find contentment doing the same thing, taking the same walks on the same leash, over and over. She can grow older, but she doesn't have to meet the challenge of changing and evolving. That's the part I envy."

"I'd take a little tranquility over dealing with right-wing legislation devastating my livelihood."

"I'm so sorry you're living through this, Evie. I wish there were something I could do."

The nature hike Evie found in the listicle is gorgeous and highly Instagrammable, but it takes only about ten minutes to cover the route, round trip. The beagle bounds around happily. Evie and I take a photo together, which I realize we've never really done. I think about Evie's selfie with one of her clients at the Grand Canyon. He and I part of the same photo album now. The brevity of the hike seems to be making Evie nervous. She keeps mentioning that she should have researched it better.

"I have an idea I want to talk to you about, something I think could be sexy," she says.

"Lay it on me."

"One of my regulars who hasn't disappeared is coming into town. He reached out to book me, and he'd like the session to involve sex. I don't have sex with clients. I book one of the workers I know for sessions when one of my clients wants to fuck."

"I didn't know that."

"I did sex work as part of dominance when I started, but I hated it. Couldn't stand it."

"Okay."

"It turns out that none of the workers who I usually work with are available ... but my client's availability overlaps with when you're here in Toronto. He'll pay for the two of us, six hundred an hour, and I'd split it with you fifty-fifty. I think we could make it really fun, actually."

Of all the discussions I expected us to have on this walk— about the evolution of play dynamics and relational identities, the queer struggle to survive this world, and likely, about us ending our relationship, the offer to be pimped out was not anything I anticipated.

A rush of thoughts and feelings runs through me. The offer feels like getting an unsolicited dick pic. My cunt gets wet because that's what my body does involuntarily when I'm exposed to something sexual that I didn't expect. As the immediate rush of the involuntary response subsides, the larger context of what's being asked of me and of who is doing the asking starts to set in.

Should I explore this as a side hustle to my low-paying arts career, since rents across Canada keep climbing? While doing sex work isn't a thing I've explored before, does having Evie present open me up to the possibility? Would it be safer for me to do sex work with Evie, since she's got her mixed martial arts training and would defend me if I needed defending? Should I consider this, especially in view of Evie's income downturn, her evaporating clients, and now with FOSTA-SESTA, her difficulty advertising for new ones? Would this be sustainable for my mental health, given the lingering trauma of having my consent breached by Broadsword and Dagger? Is this a good career for me to get into, given all the sex-related trauma in my family's fucked-up history? Is this an idea that Evie's had on her mind for a while, since it's not the first time she's suggested I do sex work? Are Evie and I still in a dom/sub dynamic, or are we lovers, or are we … co-workers? And most importantly, am I actually interested in this line of work?

"Thank you for thinking of me and presenting me with this opportunity."

Evie turns into a happy puppy herself when I don't immediately say no. While my brain processes the offer, I ask Evie questions.

"Would your client respect my they/them pronouns?"

"He's a guy in private equity overseas. I don't think he knows much about the queer community or non-binary people."

"So if I was to work with you, I'd have to pretend to be a woman."

"Like a performance role."

"I don't pretend to be a woman in my performance roles. I only play non-binary people."

"I think talking about pronouns would alienate him."

I think about how quick Evie was to tell off the bartender at Gorgeous Garbage for making an incorrect assumption about my gender and how incongruous that seems with what she's proposing now. Being misgendered in any context can be destabilizing, but given the choice between being misgendered by a bartender and being misgendered by some guy while he thrusts his dick into me ... to paraphrase *Sesame Street*, one of these things is more damaging than the other.

Evie seems happy and excited in the face of her own cognitive dissonance. Maybe it's a case of her ease with holding in what she's really feeling. Maybe because she's pitching me, she won't show any emotion that might undermine getting the answer she's looking for. Maybe she genuinely thinks that our dialogue is going well—which means we're having two very different conversations. Whatever it is, any demonstration of regard for my integrity as a trans person would go a long way at this moment. Instead, we walk in silence back to the minivan. The beagle jumps up on me as we reach the van, covering me with mud and puddle water. Evie suggests that it would have been a good idea for me to dress for the mucky conditions. I laugh at the irony of that statement.

She drops me off, and we kiss goodbye before she drives home. I ask for time to consider the proposal, and Evie grins. We plan to walk her beagle again in the evening in a couple of days. Neither of us clarifies that it'll be the deadline for me to opt in or out of her offer to employ me, but we both know that it is. We don't make plans to see each other or spend the night together otherwise. She drives back to her investment banker boyfriend's home, and I go back to the couch I'm crashing on.

Kyle leads the way to the costume section of Sexyland. They're interested in finding something fun, silly, and frilly for themself and opt for the same maid costume that's on the mannequins in the window. Then they lead us over to a wall of dildos and ask me if I'm feeling the flesh-toned ones, the glittery rainbow cocks, or the huge, veiny imports marketed with names like "Rambo." The most ludicrously big dick on the shelf is simply named, with poetic elegance, "America."

Kyle needs to feel their femme so badly. They don't post to the T-girl threads on Reddit anymore. While Reddit was a problematic forum to express their gender, at least it was a forum, and now, despite being more out, they have fewer spaces where their gender is acknowledged. While the email signature at their Aussie structural engineering job says "they/them," no one on the northern Australian coast other than me acknowledges that they're non-binary.

They're here in Sexyland to galvanize themself to survive another workweek of having their real gender shunned and erased. They're here to feel like a hot, cum-guzzling, popular slut—because they want to be loved, by a lot of people, for their femininity.

They want so badly for me to be excited about degrading them, domming them, and "making" them clean in the French maid outfit before I "make" them do other things. They want me to pick out a whip from the inventory here, bring it home, and lash their ass so it leaves marks they'll feel when they sit on their office chair on Monday. They want the pain of bruises to remind them, in the midst of their workday, that they're so much more than what their co-workers see.

They want me to jerk off while they put on a lace bra and panties and then fuck their ass hard, degrade them, muss up their lipstick, fuck their face, slap their tits, then take them for a post-play sunset walk along the Australian seashore.

They want the adrenalin, the endorphins, the rush of well-being, and the marks that linger on their skin afterward as souvenirs.

I understand all of it—because it's what I wanted and why I wanted it when I was a bottom.

Everything Kyle wants is hot, reasonable, beautiful, and necessary. The only problem is that I am not a dominant. I never was one—I just know how great doms play, and as a performer, I know how to observe, absorb, and impersonate. But the longer I set aside who I am in order to validate Kyle's gender and sexuality, the less I feel like a partner and the more I feel like a service provider.

Evie pulls up to get me, this time in a Honda Civic. I jokingly ask her how many cousins Michael has, if this is another loaner car from his extended family.

"The funny thing is, this car does actually belong to another one of his relatives."

Evie drives me and the puppy to the Toronto waterfront and parks in an empty lot next to a gas station. There's no walking trail, lamplight, or artful outdoor landscaping—just a bit of green space, dense with trees on yet-to-be-developed land, between the gas pumps, a 7-Eleven, and one of the Great Lakes.

Evie and I walk her dog into the trees. There's a nervous energy between us like we're on a first date, which is ironic, because this date is our last one.

She asks me where my thinking is at.

"I still have some questions."

"Tell me your questions, Sly."

"If your client were interested in bodies that were assigned male at birth, is this something you'd ask Michael to do with you?"

"Michael doesn't need my money."

"I get that, but that's not really what I'm asking."

"I probably wouldn't. I don't think Michael would be interested. If my client were a woman, maybe."

I hear dead leaves crackle and feel twigs snap beneath our feet. The beagle puppy runs as far ahead as her leash allows, and she pees all over the trees. I don't ask Evie to unpack all the presumptions she has around wealth, gender, assigned sex at birth, sexual orientation, and how those feed into who she thinks would or wouldn't be open to this sex work gig.

"If I meet your client and decide I'm not comfortable having sex with him, is that normal?"

"What do you mean?"

"There's still consent involved, right? I haven't met him, I don't know anything about him, so … how can I consent to having sex with him without any contact?"

"The money replaces consent."

"Okay, yes, I understand that it's sex for money as opposed to sex for desire. But I still have the right to decide who I do and don't let inside my body."

"I don't understand what you mean."

"Like, if you hired a worker, like you normally would, and she met the client but then couldn't stand the thought of having sex with him, what would happen?"

"I shrieked at her."

"What?"

"That's happened before. I booked a girl—once she got to the session, she didn't want to give my client the blow job he wanted.

I was absolutely livid. I shrieked at her, never booked her again, and never let her work out of my dungeon again."

"How could you do that?"

"What do you mean?"

"I mean, how could you do that?"

"She was unprofessional. She could have permanently jeopardized my relationship with my client. Sex work is like any other labour—if you show up to a job and refuse to do it, you don't get paid."

"Yes, but … in healthy working environments, you still get to negotiate the terms of your employment."

"Sly, when you're performing, you can't walk offstage. That level of control is given up in exchange for money."

"Every performance contract I sign has a clause that lays out what amount I lose out on if I cancel a performance. There's allowance made for the fact that live performances can't be guaranteed."

We reach the shoreline, and the lights from the city glimmer on the water. The beagle navigates a maze of large, jagged concrete fragments along the water's edge—they're bits of demolished buildings, dumped here to stop coastal erosion. Evie's mask of impassivity cracks.

"You don't understand what I do!" she shrieks.

She has watched me come more times than I can count. I've watched her do things to me and listened to her describe other scenes, with other lovers and clients, and have bordered and walked across the border of being safe and sane. I've always known how dark her imagination can get. I've always known that she's a woman who touches parts of existence most would hide from. Even with all of that said, though, it's the feeling of her shriek, as opposed to the words, that hits me in a way she's never hit me before. I feel her scream in my spine, like the harsh jolt of someone picking you up without warning or permission and then dropping you suddenly. Even though I don't blame her for shrieking, I know this feeling in my spine is not a feeling that my body will be able to forget.

We walk in silence.

Waves lap against the discarded bits of old structures.

I think about the dungeon monitor at Ashes. I picture him sitting on a piece of concrete at the shoreline, his eyes meeting mine, even in this unlit place. Once, his eyes gave me the courage to say yes when I wanted to take a risk but needed backup.

Here, imagining his eyes give me the guts to disappoint Evie.

I know how scared she is of losing more clients and that the stress of legislation from across an international border is to blame for what she's saying right now. I know that the way she is being marginalized is pushing her to anger, and if space and time were to fold, the tone of this conversation would be different. I'm disappointing someone I love, and she feels alone—but I can't bend my views around body autonomy, agency, and consent for her benefit. Space and time don't fold. We're in the spring of 2018. Trump's been in the White House for a year. The cost of life in Canada is getting scary. North America is getting scarier. We're walking a dog along Lake Ontario—and someone who loves me wants me to do something I don't want to do.

After Evie's ripped the duct tape off my mouth, I sit in her lap, bawling. The dungeon monitor comes over to us. I slide off her lap, and my ass sticks painfully to the black-vinyl couch underneath me in Ashes' cavernous concert hall. Evie chats with a human pony sitting on the other side of her. Before the dungeon monitor can say a thing to me, I reach up to him and offer him my hand. He holds it. I'm high on adrenalin, gasping for air and babbling—but I don't care, and he doesn't seem to mind either.

"I have felt so much emotional and psychological pain, for so long—for my whole life, as long as I can remember. I've always had to push it down, pretend it wasn't there, show up to life, and strive to be my best, so that no one could say what I'm capable of has been hampered or hemmed in by where I've come from, what I've seen, and what I've lived through. But it's just meant that in life, there was no real container, no place, no time, where it was safe to physicalize, name, experience, and really honour just how much pain I was in. Being a bottom was the container for my pain—the place where I could be honoured, adored, and find an appreciative audience for the hurt that I have genuinely felt in my heart every day. An audience that wouldn't shame me or be embarrassed by me, or ask me to heal and transform and be normal and be regular and be calm and be happy on their timeline instead of my own. I've been bottoming for years, and I've had great play sessions, and I've met some assholes along the way, and through all these years of play, bit by bit, I've been processing the emotional hurt that so-called vanilla life has left me with. I've been processing all the non-consensual violence that's been thrown at me, all the ways I've been neglected, all the ways I've been hated for having a cunt, for being bi, for being trans, for being born. I've been processing the harm I've endured in vanilla world through the fetish world, and it's not that this scene alone has been so powerful that it's cleansed me of all of it, but this scene, cumulatively, with every other scene, has made it so that I'm really free of a lifetime of hurt in a way I didn't know I could be, and now, I don't need to be a bottom anymore."

I'm still crying. The dungeon monitor smiles at me. Maybe he thinks I'm rambling from body chemicals. Maybe I am. I don't care.

"A cumulative, cascading catharsis."

"A catharsis that's taken me years. And now it's done."

"I'm honoured to have seen the end."

"You being here made it possible for me to trust the scene, the duct tape, to physically hurt that much, to bottom that hard and still feel safe. I wouldn't have had this catharsis without you. And I don't even know you."

"My name is Leonard."

"Leonard, I don't know how to say this with the gravity it deserves. It is very nice to meet you."

"Maybe there's something in this that's marketable," Evie says. "You're the worker who has the option to opt in or opt out with clients when you meet them. Maybe I can sell that as if booking you is a game of Russian roulette. Maybe some johns will get off on that risk and the cuckold of it."

"I'm sorry, Evie. What you do should have employee rights and workplace protections—and I know that because it doesn't, the extent to which consent can exist with clients is different. I know what you navigate in your work is extremely difficult and that it shouldn't have to be. I'm sorry for what I said, and I'm sorry for the way I said it. But—I don't want to do this with you."

Evie and I never explore the marketing angles for my career as an unreliable service provider. My work onstage in Toronto wraps up, and I head back to Vancouver. She and I share a few friendly texts before she calls me to end our relationship as dom and sub and as lovers. It's the right thing for both of us.

Whenever I think of Evie, I picture her running through a field somewhere, in tall grass, with a beagle nipping at her heels. The wind picks up the wispy bits of hair around her face as she looks over her shoulder and smiles, crinkling the skin around one eye that's blue-grey and one eye that's green. Then she turns away and runs off into the distance, chasing the sun. It's not the uncomplicated image in my mind's eye that it once was, but there's still warmth in it, and beauty.

The ways that factors outside of our control place stress on queer relationships and create tangible presumptions and pressures on trans lives are on my mind, as Kyle wraps up their Sexyland shopping. They pick up and purchase the easy-to-install under-mattress restraint system from the impulse-buy bin. They want me to pick out things too. My heart isn't in it.

I don't blame Kyle for wanting me to be a dom, just like I don't blame Evie for offering me work I don't want. They're both fumbling to keep a foothold in their own lives and trying to the turn the pipe dream of an easier tomorrow into a promise and a guarantee. This is part of the insidious harm caused by the persecution of consensual sex work, the erasure of trans and non-binary identities, and other means of discrimination that disproportionately impact queer people; as individuals, we can only endure so much discrimination before we begin to internalize it. In the process of internalizing that harm, too often we look to the people closest to us to give us a glimmer of hope. The intensity of that need—to have something we can control and to have someone who will help us maintain that control—means that sometimes, we queer people ask too much of the people we love most.

I know there are some super well-adjusted queer folk out there who grew up in gay-friendly families and haven't been conditioned into a propensity for codependence. I'm really happy for them. I watch their TikToks and subscribe to their YouTube channels. But for the rest of us queers, we have to navigate the difficult difference between compassion versus self-sacrifice, and empathy versus obligation, with skills we can only cultivate slowly, over time, by listening to our anxiety and knowing that we're never too deep into a relationship or too alone on the edge of the map to set new boundaries.

As we drive around in our shaky old hatchback, listening to Robyn soothes me. Kyle even notices it. Whenever the album *Honey* is playing, I seem to get a reprieve from the endless unease I'm carrying.

Robyn sings, and I sing along.

As soothing as the reverberating, hypnotic tones of the album are and as much as I love Robyn, Robyn is wrong. I have somebody to love, and I still have plenty of myself I could keep losing.

The days melt into each other on the northern Australia coast as the sunsets paint the sky Rothko reds and as the rust-coloured dirt picks up the yellow flecks in Kyle's big brown eyes.

They flash me their Colgate smile, but nonetheless, a distance between us builds.

I walk through the streets of small towns and baptize my own body in sweat from the forty-degree heat of the tropical buildup. When the monsoon rains come, I walk through the downpours, the only person outside in the mucky conditions. A co-worker pulls up in her minivan to ask me if I need a ride, seeing me soaked to the skin. She looks at me like I've lost my mind. I walk in and out of culture and events jobs as I waver between financial pragmatism and table-flipping frustration. I don't know what my outlets or my interests are anymore. Being a bottom isn't my therapy any longer, and being a top isn't what's true to my spirit. I become an unreliable worker, and with Kyle, I become an unreliable friend. I'm on edge, resentful, and angry.

I know certain big things about myself: that I'm bi, that I'm non-binary, and that I'm not afraid to let go of anything that doesn't serve me anymore. But outside of these beautiful certain-ties, I know more about what I want to move past than I do about what I want to move toward.

I'd accept the situation calmly if I were a trust fund kid who could just wait and see how life unfolds. But in the realities of who I am, with a partner who has come out about being trans feminine and who wants our lives in Australia to work out, I need to get up, make money, be part of communities, and have ambitions. I need to collaborate on building the new life we have here, on a continent on the other side of the planet. Sitting in a kind of listless, emo pop-punk lack of direction with a pink streak dyed in my hair doesn't feel like an option.

I approach every day with panic, like a creature under threat, keeping afloat—but just barely—in salt waters.

CAME SO CLOSE TO COMING (HOME)

The sunshine bounces off the snow and is blinding. Despite being in thick forest, we're also in the depths of Canadian winter just outside of Milton, Ontario, so all the trees are naked, leafless sentinels. I trudge through the snow in boots, snow pants, and a coat that are all too big for me. I don't own winter hiking apparel. I'm not a winter hiking person. I've borrowed everything I'm wearing from my cousins. Even though we're all related and in our twenties, my cousins are much taller than me, and most days, I still get mistaken for a young boy. The loaned gear makes me feel like I'm wearing an oversized mascot costume. Like all mascots, I'm here to hype people up and make them feel good about themselves. That's always how I feel whenever I'm around biological family en masse. It's not a role I want, so I trudge ahead of my three cousins, my uncle, and my aunt Ada as fast as I can. Inside my costume I'm clammy with the effort, despite how frigid the day is.

Aunt Ada is my father's sister. She calls out to me and does an awkward snow jog to catch up but doesn't get worn out by it. In high school in the '70s, Ada was a beast at track meets and an all-around sports star. The '70s were a long time ago, but being a jock is still a big part of Ada's personality. She coaches girls' outdoor soccer in the summer, indoor soccer when it's cold, and goes running daily. An elevated heart rate is the music that keeps her mind focused and dispels her propensity for anxiety. Exercise, that is, and Jesus. It's Christmas Day, 2015. As Ada reaches me, she tries to give me hug, but I just keep walking. She says that she's been meaning to talk to me for a long time. Without further prelude or context, she launches into describing, in graphic detail, the story of ongoing sexual abuse and rape she endured as a teenager in the home she and my dad grew up in. My dad has four siblings but only one brother. Ada tells me that it was the brother who repeatedly sexually abused and then raped her—but my granddad, her and my dad's father, was also complicit in the sexual abuse.

I look around me at the naked sentinels and over my shoulder at my cousins and uncle, bringing up the rear of our procession. My cousins smile, but I can't see their eyes through their sunglasses, so their faces are blank from the nose up, and their grins are a frightening counterpoint to what Ada's sharing. They wave at me with their big, mitted paws. Ada keeps describing the sexual abuse she endured—how many instances, what happened in each room, how often it happened, what the details of each instance were, who in the home knew what, how being abused gave her an eating disorder, how God became her salvation, and what happiness means for her today, now that she's on the other side of torture.

I look up through the branches, squint, and catch glimpses of crows flying. I lose my balance in the snow as the world shakes, like a holiday snow globe. Birds hit the ground, and the trees turn topsy-turvy, as branches become roots reaching into the clear blue sky for grounding but find none. Ada catches me and asks me if I'm all right. I don't tell her that I'm having a panic attack. Instead, I say that the sunshine got in my eyes. She tells me I should have borrowed sunglasses from my cousin Calla and tries to give me a hug again without asking if I want one. She continues her blow-by-blow account of trauma and then, just as suddenly, she turns around to rejoin her kids and husband.

The world continues to swirl in my peripheral vision. I imagine a different version of today where instead, I stayed home alone in my Toronto basement apartment. I picture the FOMO. I picture bingeing porn, jerking off, looking at bodies through the dust and gunk on my laptop screen. I picture the endless stream of other people's Christmases on Facebook and their Santa hat nudes on FetLife. I picture returning to my North York cubicle on December 27 and my co-workers pitying me. It's not an inspiring vision of what my holiday could have been, but it would have been a Christmas where I had some say over what I was feeling.

Why was I being offered this devastating information, without warning? What was the reason for Ada's unprovoked sharing, and why now? Why the explicit degree of detail in Ada's stories?

As the world flips upside down and right side up, over and over, I begin to recontextualize my entire childhood and the abuse I was abandoned to as having been shaped by violence in my father's childhood home. Ada might be sharing her story, but I'm her non-binary nibling, not some casual acquaintance. Her history is my history too.

Calla yells that we're going to do our own evening Mass around a firepit on their farm, rather than drive into town. The road conditions aren't great.

"What's the point of having a minister and a half in the family, anyway, if we can't hold Mass at home?" Calla hollers.

The ease of Ada's transition, from trauma-dumping to falling back into her picture-perfect family, is as jarring as it is to learn what happened to her. Ada acts as if we've just touched base about something innocuous. Her behaviour lets me know that this is not up for group discussion. Even though we could all sit down as a family in our adult snow pants and have an adult conversation about cycles of violence and intergenerational trauma, we won't.

Ada is a survivor, and I applaud her survival as much as I celebrate all survivors of abuse, including myself. At the same time, Ada's behaving like a creepy WASP in the most insidious, hard-to-call-out kind of way. She's shared something profoundly upsetting, triggering my sympathetic nervous system and eliciting my body's fight-or-flight response. Then, she's pretended that she said nothing out of the norm at all so that my fight-or-flight energy has nowhere to go and becomes a state of freezing. Then, she's left me in this state so I feel fucked up, pissed off, turned on, guilty, and ultimately, very alone.

As I look back at my relatives, this time it's Ada who freaks me out the most, grinning from the nose down, one mitt intertwined with her husband's hand, the other mitt waving.

She has a lot to fall back on: loving kids, a great husband who is also a church minister, assets, community, and a stable coaching career. She's a survival success story, and I'm happy for her. I just don't have any of those things. When I go home, I face the threat of Toronto reneviction alone. When I go into work, I choose between speaking up and paying my bills. When I wake up from nightmares about my stepfather, I have to remind myself that it's post-traumatic stress rather than current circumstances that make it feel like space and time are folding into terrifying forms. When I walk onstage and the spotlight hits me, it's miraculous and sad, because I need the spotlight to know that my existence might be worth something.

When it comes to all the people Aunt Ada has available to her, why hand this information to a person with little capacity left to carry it?

I'm nauseous as we finish the hike. Ada says that I must not be used to working out this hard.

"You're such a city chick!" she offers, ignoring what I've told her about my gender.

While she, my uncle Stan, and their youngest daughter, Clover, pile back into their family van, the oldest of Ada's kids, Clay and Calla, hang back with me for a moment.

"Did Mom say something to you?" Clay asks.

"Yeah. She told me that Uncle Tim raped her in their bathroom when they were both kids."

Clay and Calla look at each other and then back at me.

"We thought it might be something like that."

"Say more words, Clay, 'cause I'm pretty fucked up right now."

"She does this sometimes," Calla says.

"We think it's her way to try to build a bond."

"Like, look at what I've been through, okay, now you can trust me. Now you can tell me anything," Calla adds.

"That's kind of a messed-up way to bond with people, you guys."

"Pobody's nerfect, you know?"

"They teach you that at Harvard, Calla?"

Clay cuts in. "Okay, you two, we're the next generation here. We know better, Mom doesn't. Let's not rip each other up over how she does things. It's not worth it."

Calla nods and reaches out to touch my shoulder, like she's bestowing a blessing on me. She heads to the van to join her sister and parents.

"I'm sorry," Clay mouths at me.

As adults, Clay, Calla, Clover, and I have a different dynamic than we did as kids, when we were intermittently thrust into each other's company. My dad always referred to Aunt Ada's kids as the Garden. I could never figure out how my dad and I were perceived by his siblings and my cousins. It felt like we were the charity cases who were good enough to be invited to visit, but not good enough to get to know. There would always be two gifts on hand for my dad and I when we arrived, and they were always wrapped in fancy paper. At the same time, they were always generic gifts. A Terry's Chocolate Orange for my dad, because he liked chocolate. A bottle of bubble bath for me, because little girls love self-care. The gifts underlined that we were outsiders more than they made me feel welcome—and then I'd cycle through feeling guilty for being ungrateful for the gifts. My dad, on the other hand, would say thank you, smack the chocolate orange on the table like the TV ads said to, and eat it. I'd hold the bottle of bubble bath like it weighed fifty pounds, and at least outwardly, follow my dad's lead, pushing down how sick I felt and never mentioning how afraid I was to take a bath back at my mom's place.

Back then, the only extended family I felt okay around was Calla, with her bright, welcoming energy, her broad face covered in freckles, and her frizzy hair that was so blond, it was almost a white halo, picking up light and giving her goofy smile a benevolent authority. Even though she was a couple of years younger than me, I always looked up to her. Unlike everyone else in the extended fam jam, Calla didn't look down on me.

The reasons my relatives felt it appropriate to pity me included the fact that I wasn't growing up in a two-storey house and my parents didn't own land, homes, or driver's licences. I wasn't on any sports teams, or learning to play an instrument, or going to summer camps. I only saw my dad every other weekend, and my mom and my stepfather—whom I lived with most of the time—seemed like quintessential deadbeats. Living in shitty rentals, taking public transit, having parents who were separated, and missing out on extracurriculars—frankly, none of these things were problems, as far as I was concerned. The things that stressed me out were more life-and-death-oriented—more abuse-, depression-, and suicidal ideation–oriented. Even so, the extended family stayed wilfully naive about the real harm I faced, focused on class-related indicators of success, and treated me like I was a floundered opportunity.

My dad was the only divorced one among his four siblings, and he was also the only one still working in sales and doing shift work. All his brothers and sisters had careers and the attributes of accomplishment in capitalism. I'd like to say that my dad was the anti-capitalist of the family, dancing to the beat of his own drum, but he wasn't. He was just stumbling through life, dragged down by trauma he didn't understand, and recuperating as best as he could from the exhaustion of a protracted divorce process with my mom. He lived in a studio apartment furnished from flea markets above an Italian hair salon in a strip mall on Toronto's Dufferin Street. My dad's siblings lived in houses—some in the small towns of Ontario, where church, hockey practices, and planning winter getaways to Mexico typified life, and some on the islands off the coast of Vancouver, where good weather, caftans, and home-schooling were the norm and where excessive wealth was taken for granted.

I never asked my dad if he felt inferior to his siblings, with their two-car garages, eight-foot Christmas trees, and L.L.Bean catalogues, and maybe I should have. Maybe then, we could have spent our holidays in his studio apartment, building our rapport instead of visiting his siblings and feeling small. We'd walk into my aunts' homes in silence, while my cousins ran by with toys, hobbies, cellphones, and a sense of permanence. For them, Uncle Sid, the single dad, was coming to visit with his part-time daughter. For my dad and I, we were walking into their everyday lives, which to us were a sitcom-level fantasy.

I was always anxious about seeing relatives in my dad's extended family, especially my cousins. Adults will avoid touchy subjects, but kids will interrogate anything they don't understand. I was worried that the ugliness of my day-to-day life and my flimsy cover stories might not stand up to my cousins' scrutiny. They were just as capable of being blatant as the kids I went to school with, and there was the added danger that my cousins might have inside information.

At the same time, when I was with them, I kind of wanted to say enough to my cousins that someone might save me from my life without saying so much that I'd be beaten for it when I got home.

When I got home from court-mandated visits with my father, my mother would cross-examine every conversation I'd had while I was away. She would grill me for hours to the point of exhaustion, when it would be easy for me to slip up if I was managing too many lies. Her grilling and the way I answered her had a big impact on how many times my stepfather would yank my hair or pull me around the apartment by my hair, how many open-palmed blows to the back of my head he would give me. My mom and my stepdad were fans of injuries that would hurt but wouldn't leave obvious bruises. They relied on child support from my dad as a huge part of their monthly income, so the abuse they inflicted was shaped around making sure that I was still a sellable prize pony every other weekend. My temptation to say enough to my dad's nieces and nephews without saying too much had me on edge around them all the time. I'm sure it made me difficult to relate to.

As kids, Clay and I never connected—we were like two magnets held the wrong way around so that we repelled each other. He followed Ada's suit in school athletics and popularity. His childhood bedroom was papered with ribbons and trophies. He always had something going on, some practice to get to, some friend's birthday, some girlfriend waiting to go on a date, or some act of community service at a local outreach kitchen. He loved God, had bright eyes, was an avid reader, and was generally kind, though extremely competitive. When high school ended, he decided to take a gap year, did the middle-class ritual of backpacking through Europe, and extended that into another year of waiting tables in an oceanside bar in San Diego. By the time he came home to Milton, he was ready to share with his family that he was gay and that he'd known it to be true well before setting out backpacking.

Once he was out, Clay found me on social media, and it turned out he was living in a share house in Toronto's Parkdale, a streetcar ride away from my basement apartment. He was still on great terms with his family but also figuring out what he wanted to do with his life. In the meantime, he working as a barista, teaching himself the wooden flute, gardening, and baking bread for his roommates, who were all lesbians. Every so often, he would come see me perform at the back of some bar—spoken word pieces about femmedoms, wax play, being non-binary, licking clit, and why I didn't talk to any of my parents. We'd grab drinks afterward, and he'd laugh at my revolving door, kinky sex life, while I'd laugh at him for being too shy to message back his Grindr matches.

"I know I'll never have a boyfriend if I stay home baking bread for lesbians all the time, but I still believe in love. I still want it to be about love and lovemaking. I'm reading this great novel that says queer sex manifests offspring in another dimension, and there's a couple in the book who mark this manifestation by folding an origami animal after each time they make love. They place the animal on a window ledge in their apartment so their absent offspring can look at their world."

"Clay, even though I don't value the same things you do, whenever we talk, I feel just a little less alone."

As adults, Clay and I talk about parallel universes, exoplanets, and everything about ourselves as queer people that is not visible on this plane of existence but exists just the same. We discuss portals, talking animals, reimaginings of Eden with gay and trans couples, and the practical magic of crystals. They're easy conversations, as we talk in a language we did not cultivate with one another but share just the same. It's a bizarrely intuitive kinship, and it strikes me that this likeness is probably what kept us away from each other earlier in life. We weren't ready to process our similarities as queer souls whose fundamental desire was transcendence. Now we can talk about that, even if I pursue transcendence through BDSM and Clay seeks it out in faith and in the long, clear notes of wind instruments.

Clover is a little younger than Clay and Calla, who are only a year apart. She seems like the kid Aunt Ada and Uncle Stan decided to have when they realized they missed cradling babies. Everything about Clover is soft—the curves of her face, the silkiness of her long, wispy hair, the tone of her voice, and her pleasant personality. I have never met a human being who more closely evokes the energy of a little lamb: sweet, conflict averse, and happy.

When we were kids, I didn't ponder Clover's demureness. She was always there, whenever my dad and I would visit, but she always seemed to blend into the background—less boisterous than her brother and Calla and always smiling. As she got to be an older child, I tried to avoid her because she'd engage me in ways that weren't meant to be hurtful but carried sting just the same.

"Why do you like your hair so short, Sly?"

"My mom buzzed my hair."

"Why?"

"Because she didn't like the way I looked at her."

"That's funny."

"It was a punishment."

"My mom doesn't punish me."

One time at a park, a kid walked up to Clover and put a sticker on the tip of her nose. Clover just said, "Thank you," and carried on, completely unbothered. I was always on edge about my personal space, like a lot of people are when we don't get to set any boundaries. People who never feel safe need a wider radius and all kinds of consent check-ins, even around things that are harmless, because their fight-or-flight response is on a hair trigger, working overtime to compensate for an existing safety deficit. Watching Clover's complete calm about suddenly being touched by a stranger was just about the weirdest thing I could imagine. I really couldn't relate to or comprehend Clover because I'd never seen a human operate from such a profound sense of security.

At some point, I began imagining that Clover was contemplating the mysteries of the universe behind her quiet, peaceful smile, but whenever I talked to her, that illusion was shattered. Engaging with her felt like engaging with someone who was absent of thought—not unintelligent, just serenely empty. Somehow, she had stumbled into a kind of perpetual nirvana that monks might seek out and fail to find for their entire lives. She had found this level of tranquility within her Christian, suburban life in small-town Ontario. Maybe it was the uniformity of everything Clover had ever known that made it possible for her to exist free of anger and confusion. She was born into a cookie-cutter, manufactured neighbourhood, where every house has the same layout, floor plan, construction materials, and finishes. Only the number on the front door proved that her home wasn't sitting in a hall of mirrors. All of her friends came from similar families, and some slept in the carbon copy of her own bedroom. She was Ada's last child, and Aunt Ada absolutely loved being a mother, so Clover got the best of everything, within the confines of Protestant austerity. More than anything else, though, when you looked at her, you knew that you were looking at a kid who was loved, completely and unconditionally, and who had never at any point felt an absence of care. She wasn't grappling with great mysteries behind the scenes because she'd never had to grapple with anything. She was just utterly free of heartbreak.

Calla was the middle child and always came across as a bi-curious, open heart—which is part of why she was the cousin I felt relaxed around. She never interrogated why I was out of the loop on pop culture or questioned my off-brand, discount-bin clothes. Instead, she shared her CD collection, lent me her Tamagotchis, and sat with me on her carpeted bedroom floor, applying Claire's press-on glitter nails together in colour sets with names like Malibu Beach Nights and White Tiger. She always had an extra press-on nail set squirrelled away for sharing—and while the femminess of the press-ons didn't resonate with me, the tenderness of having each of my fingers held with love and care did. That was the kind of kid she was; she always seemed to know what people needed but didn't make a point of calling it out, so her generosity didn't make me feel poor. Instead, her presence offered a tantalizing bit of escapism and aspiration. When I was around her, I felt like if I survived past where my life was at, one day I'd end up on a beach in Malibu, at dusk, with a white tiger.

As Calla got older and came into her own queerness, she also developed a closer relationship to the church she was raised in. She grew up watching her father lead by example, in Mass and outside of it, as a minister in the United Church of Canada. Uncle Stan was a great dad and a great community leader. Even I liked Stan, and I was a pretty hard sell. Calla seemed to fuse the best parts of her dad with the other parts of her identity. Her love of God, spiritual leadership, and social progress and her comfort with her own bisexuality seemed to go hand in hand—so she didn't go to clubs or finger-fuck hot dykes in bathrooms stalls, like I was doing. Instead she wore a single earring dangling from one ear, dyed streaks of colour into her halo-like hair, talked theology with her dad, and applied to Harvard Divinity School and got in.

On visits home from the Ivy League, Calla began to codify existence more and more: there were the haves and the have-nots, the educated and the people who would never escape cycles of poverty. There was systemic violence, class war, and the violence bred of being a dog trapped in an unjust cage. Nothing she said was ever incorrect, but it began to have an edge of condescension to it—as if you needed an Ivy League education to know these realities. For me, it was a wake-up call about how sheltered Calla's own childhood had been, even when sitting on a carpeted bedroom floor with a mother who had survived rape and a cousin who was surviving ongoing violence.

"I grew up on welfare, Calla. These things you're learning about are just ... life. Please think about that when you're talking."

"I validate you, Sly. I hear your lived experience. Thank you."

She started using phrases like "lived experience" and "close reading" so often that it felt like it deserved a drinking game. I'd catch Clay's eye about it sometimes, but he'd play peacekeeper and redirect the conversation. Where Calla used to make me feel comfortable, now the press-on nails were replaced with subtle apprehension—that I felt around Calla and that Calla seemed to be feeling all the time underneath a thin veneer of performative self-awareness.

The more she progressed as a student of spirituality, the more she seemed to want to shield and defend Clover from "lived experiences." Calla became more judgmental than I'd ever known her to be, and she started looking at me like I was the dog too stupid to see the cage it was in. It didn't make sense, and I didn't like what was happening with her, but there was no way to talk to her about it. Whenever I tried, love was used as a way to deflect introspection.

"I just love my family, Sly. Including you."

As we pile into the family van after the rape reveal / Christmas Day forest hike, I sit in the back seat, hip to hip and shoulder to shoulder between Calla and Clover. The details of Ada's story roll around in my mind, loud, heavy, and out of control, as if my skull is a twisted a bowling alley, the balls are made of lead, and the finger holes have been customized to be gripped by demons.

Some of the times my dad and I visited his extended family, we went to his father's chalet instead of seeing aunts and cousins. My granddad lived on a lake in northern Quebec, a couple hour's drive from Verdun. The properties around the lake were attractive to people who wanted a good amount of land and privacy and who didn't want to deal with tourists. Donald Sutherland was one of my granddad's neighbours. The chalet itself was a simple one-storey building built on the edge of a sharp decline toward the lake, with a timber wall facing the dirt road you'd drive in on and a wall of windows facing the water. There was a second detached building on my grandfather's land, and it was his woodworking garage. The ground around it was always littered with timber shavings. It smelled of sawdust. For me, it seemed magical and mysterious. Inside the garage, my grandfather created marvels. He was a master craftsperson, creating everything from large pieces of furniture to small, intricate objects with decorative inlays and stained-glass peekaboo windows. Sometimes, when I'd look inside his garage, I'd stare at the walls of saws and cutting tools—they were the biggest, angriest, toothiest pieces of metal I'd ever seen. I was scared of them and in awe of the person strong enough to use them. The wood he used came from the land he owned, and whenever I looked at the stumps of the trees he'd cut down, I'd picture the force it would have taken, blow by blow, to knock them over. Granddad's chalet seemed like a serene, beautiful, brutal place.

There was a private bit of beach on granddad's property, and one migration season, a gaggle of geese made his beach their rest stop. The geese shit everywhere, so my granddad went down to his beach at daybreak with a golf club. He snuck up on them and beat one of the geese to death at the lake's edge while the other birds fled the scene. This was the kind of man my grandfather was: skilled, decisive, and a monster.

As a kid, this violence was normalized to me by my dad: it was what men who were men did. My dad never felt like he lived up to being a man, in granddad's estimation. He spent his whole life trying and failing to live up to his father's expectations, when he should have been ashamed of him, rather than revere him. In a lot of ways, my dad's relationship with his father and with toxic masculinity kept me from wanting to acknowledge that my own gender falls masc of centre. It wasn't until I found tender, soft expressions of boyhood in rope that I was able to allow myself that freedom. I knew masculinity was where I personally felt most calm, but it was hard to admit that when my blood relatives modelled being a man as basically being Patrick Bateman.

I never got to know granddad well or talk to him very much on our visits. I wasn't coordinated, athletically gifted, or impressive, so there wasn't much to talk about with a guy who valued excellence, self-reliance, and achievement. There was one break in the silence of our meals together, though, when I was about ten years old. My grandfather told me I didn't need to wait for my dad to bring me up to the chalet to visit.

"After all, your dad's all the way in Toronto, and we're both here in Quebec. Call me and I can talk to your mom, come pick you up at your mom's. I'll firm you up, get you swimming, kayaking. I'll make your mom a dining table—I'm sure she doesn't have one. She'll say yes to you visiting."

On the walk down the dirt road outside my granddad's chalet, my dad pulled me aside. "Don't call Granddad or come up here without me, okay?"

"Okay, Dad."

"Good."

I kicked up rocks as I walked and caught the smell of sawdust in the air.

"Your Aunt Milly's always been a bit of a kook, but she doesn't have great things to say about Granddad. She says she's been retrieving memories in therapy, but memory retrieval ... I don't know how real that is. And since then, she's dumped that therapist, so who knows."

I curled one of my hands into a fist, kept walking, and wrapped my fist in the hem of my shirt.

"She said it was stuff about Dad being sexually inappropriate with her. But I don't remember any of that from when we were kids."

I wrapped my other hand around the fist, press it into my belly, and stopped walking.

"Why are we here, if Grandad's not safe to be around?"

My dad stopped and looked at me with a face I didn't recognize, as if he were wearing a mask of his own face on top of his face for no reason.

"Because he's family."

Smooshed between Clover and Calla in the van, I think about that driveway talk with my dad and about the potential childhood sexual abuse of his sister, Milly. I think about it in relation to Ada's rape, and in relation to my dad's brother, Tim. I think about who Tim likely learned sexual violence from. I think about Aunt Milly and Aunt Ada having similar experiences in isolation, in the same home. I think about all of that in relation to my own life, and in relation to the cousins sitting on either side of me. I hold a bottle of bubble bath while my dad eats a Terry's Chocolate Orange. Our family's story is like a series of terrifying origami creatures, folded over time and threaded into a garland so it can be wrapped around a Christmas tree.

I realize just how much sense it makes that I go to events like Feast Unleashed and that I show up at James's door over and over. It makes sense that I'm drawn to bottoming and the mental state that is subspace—because "now" is never just now when you have your own trauma and the weight of intergenerational trauma all at once. Space and time are always folding. At least, through fetish, I get to control when and where the folds happen.

Smooshed between my cousins, I think about the scenarios I play out in my head when masturbating. It's not an appropriate thing to be thinking about on Christmas Day with my family, but I can't help it. The scenarios I play out in my head when I jerk off alone bear a striking resemblance to the story Ada's just told me.

My mental jerk-off fodder often involves the power dynamics of incest role play—and it always has, even before I got into age play and having daddies of many genders within fetish subculture.

Fantasizing about incest role play is not my favourite way to explore my own pleasure—in fact, I kind of hate it. But if the goal is to have an orgasm, incest role-play fantasies are my go-to. They're perfunctory and effective. The DILFY pornography that I make up and play out in my mind never involves people I know in real life, or any of my actual relatives. The scenarios revolve around me being a little girl in a fictional sitcom-like alternate reality. In these fantasies, I live in a middle-class household, on a middle-class street, in a middle-class suburb. There's a well-kept front yard with a white picket fence around it. Sometimes the time is now, sometimes the setting is the '90s, and sometimes it reaches all the way back to the '70s. The father in this fictionalized mental porn is in some kind of well-respected profession. Everything is picture-perfect in these fantasies I use to help me come—expect for the fact that daddy, and sometimes a fictionalized older brother, just happens to have sex with me behind the scenes.

Masturbating to these fantasies is the sexual equivalent of eating a Snickers bar: I crave it, and it gives me a burst of endorphins, but I know that in an ideal world, it's junk I wouldn't need.

I've always figured that these fantasies and how well they work for me has to do with the sexual abuse I endured in my mom and my stepdad's custody. Outside of the interrogations and the physical attacks, my mom and stepfather would regularly force me to look at them naked, and vice versa. They would bathe with the bathroom door hanging open. They would watch me bathe and instruct me on how to bathe, past the point of it being age appropriate and with little focus on hygiene—so I ended up showering fast and infrequently. They would make sure I was aware of when they were having sex and would leave the door to their bedroom open mid-fuck. When they started having their own kids, my mom and stepdad would tell me that it was my job to keep their kids occupied in the alley outside our apartment while they fucked, and that if I didn't keep their kids distracted and out of the apartment, it meant I *wanted* my half-brothers to see our mom and their dad fucking. It was mental warfare, sexual abuse, psychological abuse, and an ongoing attempt to integrate me into their sex life, at an arm's-length distance at first. I think the plan was to escalate the sexual abuse into group sex once my sense of normal was warped and cracked enough to break entirely.

The way my mom and stepdad tried to shape me into a victim-turned-predator by implying that I wanted my half-brothers to be subjected to the same abuse I endured was the hardest part of my childhood to reconcile. It became an insidious part of the hell that was my home. I had three little half-brothers, all toddlers turning into young boys, and all the normal amount of petulant and defiant. I'd tell them not to go inside our apartment, so they'd want to go in. I'd try reverse psychology, and they'd catch wise. I knew the door to my mom and stepdad's bedroom would be open, so whenever one of my half-brothers made a beeline out of the alley, toward the apartment, I'd do anything to stop them. I'd tackle them to keep them from being exposed to the creepy shit that had been forced on me. I'd grab them by the collar. I'd try to scare them. I'd beg, bribe, and bully them. They were little boys, and I was around twelve years old. I'd do anything I needed to do to try to protect them, knowing that at points, I was pushing and grabbing at humans half my size. My half-brothers would kick, yell, punch back at me, and call me a bitch—something they regularly heard their father call me. I knew I wasn't the monster I was trying to shield my half-brothers from, but I also knew I was going to have to become half a monster at least, to effectively insulate them from sexual abuse—and I was crumbling under the weight of trying to keep them safe while trying to survive myself. At night I'd stare at the ceiling, wondering how much of myself I would still recognize by the time my half-brothers were old enough to make their own judgments. It was and still is the worst torment I've ever been subjected to.

During this ongoing abuse, I tried to sustain my sanity through the break that was going to school and seeing my dad, who was at least more normal on the surface, every two weeks. I was always on countdown: how many days before I could get away to a dad visit, and how many hours until I could be at school again. I only had so much of this kind of survival in me, and at the age of fourteen, I reached out for help outside of my immediate and extended family. Quebec courts removed me from my mom's custody and revoked all her contact and visitation rights. My dad got a bigger apartment in Toronto, and the courts placed me there with him. Within a year, my mom and stepdad had custody issues with child protective services vis-à-vis the rest of their kids.

The last time I had a conversation with my mom was over the phone when I was fourteen, with two police officers standing next to me. It was during the messy period after affidavits had been filed, but before any judge had made a ruling yet about where I had to live. My mom was still technically my legal guardian, so she called the cops about why I'd left home—and I found myself sitting in a police precinct. After getting to know me for a few hours, the officers decided to put me on the phone with my mom so I could talk to her about whether or not I *wanted* to come home. They stood beside me and listened as my mom told me I was sick little girl with emotional problems, that I needed help because I was psychologically unwell, and that she was praying for me.

An officer took the receiver from me and hung it up while I burst into tears.

"I don't know you well, but you don't seem sick to me," the other cop offered.

In the van ride back with Aunt Ada and her family, I think about these experiences of abuse and gaslighting. At the same time, I begin to develop a new understanding of my Snickers bar masturbation scenarios.

I've always thought that my jerk-off fantasies had to do with the abuse I personally endured and how visceral and familiar that experience is in my body—but recast in a better income bracket. I always thought it was as if I couldn't connect to my sexuality without it being connected to abuse, but I *could* imagine other parts of my childhood being better. I figured I was just imagining away the poverty and building a middle-class alternate reality in my mind as a way to the reclaim other aspects of a childhood I never had. Goodbye to being pitied, to arriving at school dirty, to the depression of growing up in Verdun, and to talking to internet creeps in the school library. But as Ada sits in the front seat, singing along to a hymn blaring from the dashboard, I realize that my Snickers bar fantasies aren't a complete fabrication—because what I imagine, when I need to come, is what my Aunt Ada actually lived.

For as long as I've been masturbating, I've been imagining something eerily similar to my aunt's life as a teenager in the '70s. She grew up in a middle-class house, on a middle-class street, in a nice neighbourhood, with a dad who was a skilled, decisive provider for his family—and dad and brother abused little girls in the family behind the scenes.

How did I know this story before I knew it consciously?

Was it an oddly perceptive guess, based on a quick conversation I once had with my dad in my grandfather's driveway? Was it just a coincidence? Was I just aware of incest porn, and is it just that too many kids are sexually abused at home in this fucked-up world? Or did my intuition come from somewhere deeper and feed into my fantasies as the only arena in which I could physically and emotionally process my family's history?

We pile out of the van at my aunt and uncle's hobby farm. I have the remaining brain capacity of a zombie. All these questions and realizations overwhelm me quietly, while my cousins act like it's a typical Christmas Day. I respond in one-word answers when I'm asked questions, perform tasks when I'm asked to do things, and the rest of the time, I just try to breathe. Uncle Stan piles wood logs into an outdoor firepit and crumples up old newspapers for kindling. Calla pulls some day-old hot dog buns out of a cupboard to consecrate as the body of the saviour. Clay calls me over to the eight-foot-tall Christmas tree and shows me where a Progress Pride Flag ornament is nestled in the green needles. I take it all in, but I'm not part of it. They may as well be a family on the other side of a TV screen.

We sit together on tree stumps perched in the snow at dusk. My uncle ministers evening Mass while we huddle around the flames. I hold a piece of consecrated stale hot dog bun in my mouth until it starts to melt. Uncle Stan says, "This is my body," and I tune out the rest. I focus on just that fragment of the blessing— this is my body—and acknowledge my racing heart. I let the cold of the winter air pass through me.

After dinner, Clover climbs onto the couch to keep me company and ask me questions.

"Clay says great things about your performances. Can you show me anything?"

I have photos from a recent performance of a narratively elliptical show that jumps around the timeline of my life and explores my existential need to find integrity, self-esteem, and cohesion.

"There's nudity in it—I'm the performer, so I'm naked. It's definitely mature subject matter around sex and identity. If you're cool with that, I can show you."

"I'm cool with that." Clover smiles. "You're my family, and I love you."

I flip through the performance photos on my phone, images of me standing naked in front of audience members, asking them if I can try on their shoes. It's all a bit trite and obvious, and I'm embarrassed about my career as an artist as I show it to my cousin. She's probably going to do something more grounded with her life than play make-believe and put on strangers' footwear.

"What's happening in this photo?" Clover points.

In it I'm on the floor naked, tied into child's pose with a long, black power cord as the stand-in for jute. The power cord is connected to a microphone. Instead of amplifying my voice, the microphone is wedged between my teeth, gagging me.

"This part of the show is about the clarity I find and the inhibitions I lose during rope bondage sessions."

"What's rope bondage?"

"As part of the way I explore sex and sensuality, sometimes I let people I trust tie me up, with a lot of care and consent check-ins, as part of the way we share and explore pleasure."

As midnight rolls around, my relatives start to peel off to their bedrooms, and I curl up to sleep on the couch beside the Christmas tree. I feel like less of an emotional wreck after hanging out with Clover. Maybe tomorrow morning, I'll even take another walk with Ada to begin some kind of meaningful dialogue—or at least to have a debrief.

When everyone's gone to bed, Calla comes back into the living room, with its vaulted ceiling, huge fireplace, and large windows facing out into the woods. She sits on the couch near my feet.

"Can you believe that this is your family home? I know Harvard's Harvard and you've always lived in nice houses, but look at this place. It's *Architectural Digest*. It's spectacular."

"It can be your family home too."

I well up a bit. It would be really nice to have someplace I could always come home to.

"Can I talk to you about something?"

"Mm-hmm."

"Tonight, you were showing Clover some photos?"

"Yes. From my last show. The one Clay came to see."

"And you talked to her about bondage?"

"Yes I did, in gentle terms."

"Sly, Clover's really innocent."

"I told her there was nudity and mature content around sex and identity before I showed her anything. I asked her if she was okay with seeing nudity and mature content first."

"I know. Even if she says yes, she doesn't understand what she's saying yes to."

"Hang on, she's an adult. She's twenty. She asked me about my work, and I gave her content warnings, like I do with audiences."

"She's a very young twenty."

"What does that mean?"

"She was uncomfortable with it."

Outside, a crow hits the ground again. My chest starts to tighten.

"Calla, you know what your mom told me today. You've seen me being completely out of it. I didn't know I needed to shield a twenty-year-old woman from her own ability to give informed consent—especially given what Ada dumped in my lap. I told Clover what was in the photos before I showed them to her. I wasn't showing her my actual sex life. I showed her photos of some provincially funded theatre."

"I'm just letting you know, she was upset."

"I can talk to Clover about what she's feeling."

"I talked to her already. Now, I just want to check in with you. Like, for the future."

"About?"

"What is and isn't crossing the line."

"The 'pobody's nerfect' line?"

"Hmm?"

"The implied line that I'm supposed to see or feel or something around what is and isn't appropriate to share with adult family members?"

"I think you should be guided by who the specific person is that you're talking to."

"I understand context, Calla. I'm a real person who lives and functions in the world. I'm familiar with the basics of interpersonal interaction. From context, I picked up on Clover's naïveté. She asked me what was happening in the show in one of the photos, and I toned down my answer substantially from what I would say to a funding jury or peers who have sex lives."

"I'm just letting you know what she felt and that she talked to me."

"No, you aren't."

"You don't have to be angry. You are welcome here."

"I don't feel welcome."

We're quiet for a moment. Time and space fold. Calla's halo-like hair picks up sunlight and glows as she squishes a press-on nail onto my pinky.

"What's the context for your mom telling me about Uncle Tim today?"

"I don't know."

"You seem to know the story, and Clay seems to know the story already. Does Clover know?"

"No, she doesn't. Mom doesn't want her to know."

"She's innocent."

"Exactly."

"And that's a virtue that needs protecting."

"It's just … a rare quality in this world."

"So that's why I had to listen to the details of rape today? Because I grew up in a fucked-up home, so I don't need protecting?"

"You have the muscles to carry certain things."

"I didn't choose to develop those muscles. That choice was taken away from me."

"But now you have them."

"No, that's not how it works. I don't get to have less choice about what I take on now just because I had no choice in what I took on then. I don't have more capacity to carry horror stories because I've carried them my whole life—I have less capacity."

"If you don't want to hear about sexual assault, then why talk to Clover about bondage? Are you using Clover to get back at Mom?"

"I talked to Clover about a consensual act, not an act of violence."

"The word 'bondage' has certain connotations."

"It can, but what I described was a consensual, intimate practice. I made that clear."

"Clover's too young to understand that."

"She might not currently understand, but she isn't too young to have the capacity to."

"If it sounds violent to her, it is violent."

"But the difference is consent."

"She doesn't understand that."

"Don't you think she deserves to understand?"

"She'll figure out what she needs to understand in her own time."

"But I've been abused, so I can hear about rape any old day, whether it's what I need to understand or not."

"What Mom shared is understandable, and like, you of all people should be more compassionate about it. She hurts, and

226

she doesn't know what to do with that hurt, and sometimes she's messy with it. But she means well, and I think she thought it would help you feel, like, closer to her, and to all of us."

"I'd feel closer to all of you if Clay weren't the only person here who used my pronouns."

"Mom's a different generation."

"Everyone else here deserves leeway and compassion?"

Calla starts, stops, and takes a deep breath before continuing.

"Mom's trying to heal—herself, and others. You know I'm queer. I go to as many queer events as you. At Harvard there's a broad focus on the intersection of queerness, non-traditional lifestyles, and spirituality. I have friends in open relationships. Clay's told me about your performance work, and like, I love your self-expression. I love it. But here at home, there's a way we do things. That's how Clover's been raised, and that's how she continues to live."

"So I'm welcome here, but with an asterisk."

"We don't talk about our sex lives, but yes, we can talk about bad things that have happened."

"But not with everyone."

"I guess … no, not with everyone. Not for now, anyway."

"So if I were a survivor who found God, I'd be free to talk about that—as long as Clover's not in earshot. But as a survivor who has found BDSM, I'm not the right kind of survivor."

"It's not that serious, Sly. There are just things we do and don't say."

Uncle Stan drives me to a Greyhound terminal the next day to catch a bus back to Toronto. The roads have been salted, and I listen to the plunk of it picked up by wheels and sent hurling into the van's chassis. Stan and I are cordial but quiet. It's the last time I hang out with the Garden.

Real life is so much stranger than fiction and so much more banal, simultaneously. The pretenses and hypocrisies of it aren't thought out, and they don't accomplish anything productive. The casting of roles is arbitrary, and the cost of turning down a role is high. On Christmas Day with my family in Milton, I wasn't interested fulfilling the role of being the troubled relative who has to carry the trauma of others while concealing how I metabolize my own. I don't view myself as damaged goods, and I don't think of people with less trauma as being an enviable or rare tier of society. No one is tainted by survival, and no one's a saint for being lucky.

The lessons we implicitly learn as kids in homes with abuse don't serve us in adulthood. Our childhood survival strategies of shielding and concealing only served a specific space and time. If we don't let those strategies go as adults, the world will keep being a place that's uglier for survivors than it is for predators.

I appreciate knowing why my dad never looked too closely at what happened to me as a kid in the twenty-six days a month that I spent in my mom's custody. It's helpful to understand that I was abandoned to violence because my dad had been trained in his childhood to ignore it. That knowledge doesn't translate to forgiveness, but it does make the past less confusing.

The mental images of Ada's explicit descriptions live on in my mind and come up for me at the most inconvenient moments—at job interviews, when I'm trying to hook up, or when I'm alone in the shower.

I still masturbate to fantasies about incest role-play dynamics when I'm close to coming and need a fucked-up oomph to get me the rest of the way there. I'll never fully know if these fantasies come from my family's history, if they're a reimagining of my own experiences with better decor, or if my brain has just cobbled these scenarios together from sexualized media and scary stories.

Space and time fold. I hold the origami shapes of it as best I can as they flatten out only to reform in my fingers again. Sometimes it feels like I'm the one making decisions and doing the folding. Sometimes it seems like it's the universe itself that's guiding my hands.

TRANSLAND

I'm at the bank of an artificially constructed lake, in Lumphini Park. The water is still and bright green from being rich with algae. At the edge of the park, the tops of palm trees meet the skyline of Bangkok's office towers. I barely move in the midday heat of the city, and sweat pours out of me. I'm holding a bag of pad Thai fresh from a street vendor's wok, and for the moment, I'm on my own. I've fallen in love with Bangkok, without hesitation or reservation. It feels good to know that I can still fanboy. It's the last day of 2019. Despite the inspiring surroundings, the end of the decade is stalking my movements, tickling my heels, and relentlessly whispering in my ears, "What's next for your life?"

Kyle and I are staying in a cheap hotel in the Silom district of the city, with low ceilings, bright-yellow walls, and windows facing out on to the hustle of Sala Daeng Road. During the day, Silom is a business area. The narrow streets are an intricate dance of food carts, cars, pedestrians, and an ongoing act of will, on the part of city workers, to maintain and repair infrastructure in a capital that has no capacity to close, pause, or slow down. There's a constant throng of motorcyclists zooming through the streets, alleys, and veins of the city. They move faster than anything else and are the lifeblood that keeps the city going—lifeblood dressed in Adidas track pants, flip-flops, and bobblehead helmets. Most of them are independent contractors working for Grab, Bangkok's version of Uber, and they deliver food, packages, and people who sit sidesaddle on the back of their motorcycles and hold tight to their drivers' ribs. Their bare toes are held in the air above gas pedals as they navigate the organized chaos. The trick to traversing Bangkok is to stay alert, be present, and move with radical grace.

Everywhere in Silom, families of wild cats call the streets home. They are feral neighbourhood cohabitants, and all the shop owners put out water and milk for them. Pragmatically, they are a line of defence against rats and vermin. Philosophically, cats are entrenched in Thai culture and signify luck or the lack thereof. In Silom, the kitties know their value and worth in their world. They're social and used to being around humans. Kyle takes out cash at an ATM on Sala Daeng, and a group of soft kittens climb over their shoes, nuzzle at their ankles, and break their soft heart in the nicest way.

"Little cuties!" they cry, as the crouch down to talk to the cats. "I will give you anything you want!"

While Kyle likes a hard spanking, at the end of the day, they always fall in love with sweetness.

At night, Silom is a party district. The consumption of alcohol is strictly regulated in Thailand; its sale is illegal in the morning and carefully restricted in the afternoons. As the sun sets on Silom, the name of the game is to pick up a big bottle of Chang beer at a 7-Eleven and down it with dinner at one of the hundreds of street food vendors that emerge for the evening up and down the district's laneways. If you aren't an asshole about it, the cops are happy to ignore open drinking on the street, so it's a very civilized open-air cafeteria. In Silom at night, it's an open-air cafeteria of mostly queer people.

The district is the epicentre of Bangkok's sex tourism industry and gay night life. The plastic stools and fold-up laminate tables, set up ad hoc on the roadside, become a collective of LGBTQ locals and visitors. Alongside street food are tables of garments for sale. Do you need a jock strap for the party you're headed to, or a last-minute red-fishnet bodysuit? Not a problem. No one's shy or scandalized at night in Silom. Hedonism and convenience stores are everywhere, as is the availability of intimacy, dominance, and submission for hire. The potted plants in the area participate in the vibe, with signs jammed into their earth, begging, "Please, Do Not Pee On Me." If the daytime streets of Silom are an organized chaos, at night, they're a polite free-for-all. Everyone's looking for pleasure, excitement, and a story to tell.

The more indecent a night you're looking for, the narrower the alleys you walk down get. It's as if the city uses its own body language to let you know: don't walk the path less travelled unless that's really where you need to be.

We're here in Bangkok while Kyle's employer is closed for the holidays. We're both grateful for a break from northern Australia, where small-town attitudes have us climbing the walls. More and more, we've been getting through the workweeks by getting obsessed with *Drag Race Thailand*, which finished its second season earlier this year. Unlike its US counterpart, which took about a decade to get past being transphobic, *Drag Race Thailand* has always had openly trans and non-binary contestants. The winner of season 2 is a trans woman named Angele Anang.

The success of someone like Angele means a lot to Kyle, who until recently only ever presented publicly as a trans feminine person under masks at fetish events and anonymously online. In their day job as a structural engineer, Kyle's email signature reads "they/them." To Kyle's Australian colleagues, those pronouns don't mean anything.

The work culture of structural engineering in Australia doesn't include many trans people—or at least, not many trans people who are out about it. Kyle has skills that the workforce needs, so they aren't shunned and excluded from employment for being trans or non-binary. Instead, Kyle's colleagues go out of their way to actively ignore Kyle's gender. It's not an air of inclusivity or a situation where gender is irrelevant. The sense is that, because Kyle is educated, talented, and very good at their job, they can't possibly be trans—they just have eccentricities. The more Kyle pushes the envelope with the clothes they wear, the length of their hair, and the way they express themself, the more their colleagues work to implicitly erase and explain away what Kyle is very clearly articulating.

If Kyle wore a T-shirt on casual Friday that read, "This is what a woman looks like," no one at their office would think they were saying that they were a trans woman. Their colleagues would do mental gymnastics to avoid the obvious and decide Kyle was being ironic, making a joke, or expressing solidarity with feminism, or something. The codified norms of Kyle's industry mean that it doesn't matter how blunt they get about who they are: it will still be strategically overlooked, misinterpreted, and recontextualized so the codified norms of the environment don't have to evolve or change.

It's a bizarre manifestation of transphobia where the trans or non-binary person themself isn't shunned because their know-how is needed, so the shunning they experience is restricted to the very nature of who they are, while their skills are still issued fat paycheques. It's sort of the labour force equivalent of when I was dating straight guys who knew that I identify as non-binary but treated my gender like it was a verbal tick to put up with on the way to getting their dick licked. What Kyle's living through at work is much more difficult than my phase of dating straight Vancouverites, though. It's a lot harder to contemplate quitting a lucrative career you've worked for than it is to ghost some douchebag you met on Tinder.

Kyle's situation illustrates why inclusion isn't satisfied by having a foot in the door or a seat at the table, and it illustrates how often trans people in the workforce are only allowed to be trans on paper.

Kyle is aware of how many trans and non-binary people never get the opportunity to work in a lot of industries at all due to economic, educational, and social discrimination, so they're alone in a narrow alley with no peers in sight, walking a path less travelled. They keep trying to be grateful for the rarity of the position they're in, but more and more, they feel like being on their own in the narrow alley is not the place they want to be.

As we sit on a couch that came with our rental and watch Angele Anang get crowned, for Kyle, it's about more than seeing someone like us represented in the media. It's a representation of a world where Kyle could be successful and trans, instead of being successful despite being trans. It's a world where trans and non-binary identities are part of the commonplace spectrum of gender diversity, and one where no trans person in any work environment is there alone. On season 2 of *Drag Race Thailand*, there are many trans performers in the workroom, which means there isn't a single trans narrative or a single trans person bearing the weight of representing an entire community. As a result, the trans competitors are just competitors, and, go figure, in a more equitable context, all the trans women on the season do really well. It's a Drag Race workroom where gender diversity isn't selectively ignored and where it isn't interrogated or questioned by the cisgender people in the room, either. None of the competitors are having a learning moment about gender, and none one's identity is exploited as a teachable moment. For Kyle, it's a vision of real inclusion, as opposed the workrooms they sit in, where microaggressions are constant. They're getting sick and tired of diversity being an optional lunchtime seminar, rather than an employment prerequisite. They need trans and non-binary peers, idols, and mentors.

All of this is on my mind as I sit alone at the edge of a lake in Lumphini Park. I've been tracking Angele Anang's movements via her social media. From everything that's online, it appears she's in the Maldives. There's no indication that she's been booked for any New Year's Eve parties here in Bangkok, but my instincts are telling me that she'll be here somewhere in this city for the start of a new decade. In any case, I'm hoping it's my instinct telling me that we will find Angele. I might not be looking to give a spanking or to get one here in Thailand, but like everyone else in Silom, I am still looking for a good story. I want a narrative that makes sense of where I am in life and makes sense of the inner turmoil Kyle is working through. If life can't make sense to me right now, then I'd at least like for Kyle to have a profound moment here in Bangkok. I'd like the universe to guide them to where they need to be while they sit sidesaddle and hang on tight to their driver's ribs.

For both of us, as a t4t couple, all of our resilience, hardships, and survival have to be going toward some meaningful end. They just have to be.

"I have so many lovers, Sly, but I just can't stop myself. Where does it end, and what's it all for?"

My bare ass rests on the tatami flooring of the Shibari Salon while James lights up a cigarette. He's clawing his way back into the life he's been trying to live, despite the grief of having to leave Canada. All last-ditch attempts to extend his visa have failed.

He's clawing his way back to self-awareness after a period of relapse. He's been burning spoons in his bathtub, bailing on teaching, and vacillating between grabbing meals at a church soup kitchen up the street and living on fries and fried chicken. He's made enough money running his small bondage business that he hasn't lost the lease on this studio in the midst of injecting stimulants and falling off the map. But during this recent relapse, he tied onstage at the Black Mask Bondage Extravaganza while high and terrorized and terrified the rope bottom he was tying. James is my friend, but he is not always a good person. I know it, and he knows it.

I can't stand by some of the things he has done. I don't know why he's shown me the benefit of more caution and care than some of the other rope bottoms he plays with. Over the year that I've known him, whenever he relapses, he ejects me from his orbit, and we reconnect when he's closer to Earth again. I appreciate that he keeps me away from him when he's at his least reliable, but I don't trust that I'll always benefit from this special treatment.

In his latest stretch going incommunicado, I was on the Queen streetcar when I looked out the window and saw James coming out of the Queen Street Kentucky Fried Chicken. He looked like absolute shit. His long black hair was still braided down his back, like always, but he looked drawn, gaunt, and angry. The thick skin of his face was cold and still. While he always looks like he's searching, coming out of the KFC, the soul was missing from his movements, as if his searching was being driven by a force other than his spirit, and there was no joy in it. It was the only time I saw with my own eyes the part of his existence that he protects me from. The rest of the time, I just hear from his stories about the mundanity and bleak chaos of what he gets up to when he's high.

I know that James is a fire I am drawn to. We both look at the world and observe its surrealism, cruelty, triumphs, and petty ironies for what they are. We both see people for who they really are a little too clearly to feel at ease around most of them. The deepest thing James and I share is that how we perceive the world is what keeps us from feeling at home in it.

We're both facing the fact that, for all the searching we do, at the end of it all, we might end up with nothing.

I know that the longer I am in James's life, the more probable it is that I'll get burned. He's leaving soon, so our story has an arbitrary ending. We don't discuss staying in touch. There are no nostalgic plans for the future. It's not who are to each other.

As we get ready to tie, James tells me his greatest fear: that in order to be well and stay well, he'll have to give up his sense of wonder.

"I don't know who I'll be if I stop manifesting awe."

I tell him my greatest fear: that in order to be well, I'll have to let go of being angry.

"Who would I be without my rage?"

"I don't know how to stop making people amazed and feeling I owe the world amazement. You don't know how to trust your strength without pain or without feeling it tested." James smiles. "Awe and anger. Yin and yang. Opposites attract, sweetie."

He tells me to pick out some music, to drown out the Hideaway.

He flicks on the LED spotlights sitting in the corners of the suspension rig, throwing purples and greens across the room. I plug my phone into the speaker on the floor, and put on some Hundred Waters. I put on their song, "Down From the Rafters." James tells me to get long reams of rope down from the wooden staff where they hang, organized by length like a jute curtain or a bondage buffet. I'll miss the seediness of the Shibari Salon and its practical elegance. The sound of a delicate flute, sharp, clean, and hopeful, layers on top of the bass pounding upward from the bar downstairs. I pull pieces of rope from their hanging place, and the friction sends fine bits of jute dust up into the air. The fragments float down slowly and catch in my nostrils. They make the room smell like earth. James stubs out his cigarette in an ashtray. I watch the smoke dance itself into memory. The smallest amount of ash touches his rough, callused fingers.

I'm already slipping, and James hasn't even put rope on me yet. Somewhere, its Ash Wednesday. Somewhere there's a thumb marking an X on my third eye. Somewhere there's a mosh pit lit from below where everyone dances in unison and where every foot on the dance floor lifts into the air simultaneously. Space and time ... what is it ... what is it that they do again?

"This music pick—it'll really take you where you need to go."

"James. Subspace."

"I see where you're headed. I haven't even started with you yet."

I melt into a soft clump of human being on the floor. My focus softens. The delineation of forms and objects in the room gets fuzzy, but other sensations get stronger. I can feel the millimetres of air closest to the surface of my skin like a cold, shimmery aura. It's a region of space time I lose awareness of everywhere else, except for here with James, when we tie alone together. Here, I can feel the movement of the atoms that I think of as me and the point at which those atoms meet the world.

It's intoxicating.

"I've been thinking about what to do with you tonight, because this might be the last time we play. It has to be different. I have somewhere I want to take you."

I look through green and purple light at my naked body made of microscopic vibrations, and at the person who makes me see myself as a series of vibrations.

"Yes, please, James."

He kneels on the floor and spreads his big hands wide over where reams of rope lie on tatami. As his palm touches jute, his fingers snag the bonds and swish back and forth, whisking every inch of rope toward his body.

Rope is an uncooperative medium to work with, as an artist, because it only looks bold and compelling when under tension, but it has almost no tension of its own. It's up to a rigger to use knots, gravity, the muscles in their back, and the muscle memory in their fingers to turn flimsy, limp strands into firm, fascinating structures.

I've never seen anyone move with rope the way James does. He moves like he understands the way jute wraps around itself in each piece of rope, creating its own small amount of inherent tension, and he knows how to use that small amount of inherent energy to make rope move like water, or he can build on that small amount of inherent energy to make rope move like a spring-loaded cannon. In kink circles, people would say that Sakura has masterful rope management technique, and that's an accurate way to describe what he does. But emotionally, watching Sakura handle rope is a lesson in virtuosity. It's like watching a ballet dancer stacking muscles with extreme precision to move a body in ways it wasn't made to move—and making that complex process appear to be second nature. He's more than a rigger—Sakura is a fucking rope God.

He's about a foot and a half taller than me and twice as broad. He knows I like sting pain and that all manner of skin scrapes are wanted and welcome. He reaches out and pulls me toward him. I feel every firm strand of interlocking tatami fibre in the flooring drag against my skin. Another rope top might rub their hands over my body to warm me up for rope. With James, the environment is a sex toy. The room is as much part of our rope scene as our orifices. By pulling me across tatami, he warms up my skin, letting the floor do the work. James deals in practical elegance.

He pulls off his shirt and growls at me, like a lion ready to play-fight with his cub. My body softens, my shimmery aura dips a degree, and any tension left in me relaxes and unfurls. I'm in the presence of someone big, strong, and talented, and they're going to set me free.

James rolls me flat on my back, scoops up my legs, and rocks me back and forth in happy baby pose while he growls at me. I cub growl back. His hands are so big, he can grasp both of my ankles in one hand, between a dexterous thumb and a pinky. He shows me the ring finger on his other hand. He's wearing a small, round yin-yang ring. He keeps eye contact with me, one hand folding my legs and pressing my ankles into my torso, the yin-yang hand raised to his mouth. He licks his ring finger like a big cat and slips it into my cunt. I feel the bass from the Hideaway reverberating through the yin-yang ring against my lips.

The suddenness of his finger inside me isn't about making me come. It's about eliciting radical awareness. It's remembering that we're always permeable. The permeability of our bodies is what gets oxygen into our bloodstream. To be breathing is to be penetrated. I scream into the rib cage of the suspension rig. We're creature within creatures, inhaling, exhaling, and growling in the belly of a larger beast.

James pulls his ring finger out of me and reaches for jute.

His rope criss-crosses up and down my shins, tying my happy baby legs into each other and into my torso. He rolls me, roughly, over the jute on my legs like I'm a human sausage. The bonds dig into my flesh. The smaller fibres of the jute scratch and scrape at my nerve endings, almost imperceptibly. I love our rough floor play. I growl and moan like an ugly little beast while James rolls me, encases me with rope, and ties off the rope to immobilize my legs.

He flicks a second piece of rope up into the air like it's an extension of his own body. He rolls me around on the floor, over the bonds, so that every part of my shins, outer thighs, and lower back is scraped, massaged, bruised, and will be lined with ligature marks that will take hours to fade. He leans over my little body, growls in my ear, and bites between my neck and shoulder with a wide, open jaw, like a cat picking up its baby. I scream, growl, and squirm my legs against the jute they're caged in. I feel James's lion nose against my cheek. His long black braid slips over his shoulder and drapes over my body.

He takes my wrists, one at a time, and uses the second piece of rope to tie them to my ankles. I'm a completely immobilized ball, rope braiding my arms into my legs and my legs into my umbilical cord. I'm a small thing, such a small thing, as James rolls me over tatami again and my face scrapes against the straw tatami fibres. Rope dust swirls around the room. I feel the tropical sun that the jute grew beneath, I smell the wet earth, I feel the heat in James's arms, and I see snow falling through a window on the streets of Toronto. I am everywhere the rope has been, I'm ancient and I'm new, old and young, awake and shimmering. James slips his fingers between the rope on my back and my spine and ever so slightly tugs the rope away from my surface. This tiny movement feels huge, as it changes the tension of the rope all over my body. The pressure and abrasiveness of the rope on my shins intensifies, making microscopic cuts in my skin. A wave of endorphins floods through me. I scream into the tatami. I'm on my face on the floor, so I can't see James smile. But I can feel it.

Suddenly, I'm in my body and outside of my body at the same time. I can feel every millimetre of where the rope meets my skin. I can feel the warmth, contentment, and endless safety of being a baby in the womb. I can feel my third eye pressing into the mat. I can feel the bass from the Hideaway downstairs thumping into my third eye and into the rope around me, like a heartbeat— and I can also see James, as if I'm an insect on the ceiling above him. I can see his shoulder blades moving with strength and ease under his lion fur. I can see the focus in his dark eyes and the pleasure and wonder it brings him to make people feel so wild and ecstatic. I can see the rise and fall of his ribs and the rise and fall of the Japanese characters etched down his rib cage. I can see the suspension rig itself, expanding and contracting as it breathes around us, a living animal so vast that most of the time, we forget we're inside it. I can feel my breath against the floor and the small, humid corners of my lips. There are worlds within worlds. I flip across the planes of existence like they're pages in a book. I'm becoming nothing and everything. I've felt this feeling before, and it never stops feeling new.

James rolls me onto me back, kisses me with his big, rough lion tongue, and reaches for a nearby bag. He pulls out a candle the colour of old blood. It's cone shaped, narrowest at the base, and widest at the top, where the wick protrudes from a big, dark-red circle.

"We've never done any wax play. This candle will melt down into itself because of the shape of it. The hot wax will only drip out if the candle is tipped over. This is where I want to take you. Are you interested?"

I look up at him through the green and purple light. I nod my head, yes.

"Do you want to know more, or should I show you and we'll check in as we go?"

"Show me."

James moves quickly. He grabs a piece of rope, throws it over a beam in the suspension rig, and catches it as it falls down on the other side of the beam. He ties the rope into the binds circling the widest part of my left hip. I'm on the floor, but I'm anchored to the ceiling. He grabs another rope, throws it over the beam above us again, and ties this second suspension line into the binds circling the left side of my ribs. He does this twice more, anchoring into my right hip and the right side of my ribs. There are four suspension lines reaching up from my body to the rafters.

He stands up and pulls on the suspension lines connected to my ribs one at a time, using them to lift my ribs just a few inches from the floor. He ties knots in the suspension lines, so they'll hold my rib cage elevated after he lets go. I'm in a partial rope suspension.

He looks me in the eye while he stands over me to make sure I'm listening.

"I'm about to do the same with your hips so you'll just be floating above the tatami. Are you ready?"

A wave of endorphins rushes through me again. I have never been so ready for anything.

"Yes, please."

He pulls at the last two suspension lines quickly in succession, lifting my hips off the floor by just a few inches. The whole balance of weight, strain, and pressure in my body, encased in the rope, changes. The thing about gravity is that it presses your body into rope with the same force, whether you're a few inches from the ground, or eight feet in the air.

I'm in a full rope suspension.

He checks my hands to make sure I still have sensation and movement. I grasp and squeeze his thumb with each of my hands like I'm a baby. He rests his palms against my feet. I wiggle my toes for him.

"All green, sweetie?"

"Greenest green, Sakura."

I play with the movement in my neck which, other than my fingers, toes, and face, is the only part of my body that can substantially move. I feel my spine hanging. Planes of existence fold. I feel my lion cub face, and I feel teeny tiny cocks sprouting from each of my vertebrae pushing through the surface of my skin to form a mane of little hard-ons. I gestate anew in a perverse womb, hanging in the air.

James walks around me and kneels by the top of my head. He gently guides the back of my head to rest on his knees. I feel the rough denim on his thighs against my little dicks, at the top of my spine. He picks up the candle again and grabs a lighter. My head rests in his lap, my body hovering above the floor, and all the cocks along my spine reach out in agony, begging for a mouth or an orifice. He places the narrow base of the candle in my mouth. He lets it go, tentatively, to make sure my lips can hold the candle upright.

I can hold the candle upright in my mouth. I can do this. I'm doing this.

James ignites the lighter but holds for a moment—our consent code. I can opt out of this offer and spit out the candle.

I don't spit out the candle.

He lights the wick.

I watch the flickering dance of the flame at the top of the blood-red tower held between my teeth.

Time and space slow down as I watch the candle burn.

James's hands hover on either side of my face, ready to catch the tower if it falls. I keep watching the flame. I can see James's face, hovering out of focus, above me in the quiet, purposeful stillness of this intense and elaborate moment. In my whole life, I never dreamed I'd hang in the air, half an animal and half a many-cocked creature, with my mouth full of fire.

Within this stillness, in the inches between myself and the ground, and in the inches between James's hands and the candle, I am free. I have no past, no future, no worries or responsibilities, no roles I have to play or people I have to be, no wants, no needs, no definitions, no fixed forms, no desire, and no dread. For a moment, I either exist in some full, interdimensional capacity, or I cease to exist completely.

Kink is such a strange form of alchemy, in which sensation, commonplace objects, intention, imagination, and a willingness to touch the unknown combine to step outside of what's possible and step toward what is true.

James's hands are so callused from years of rope that he doesn't need to lick his fingers. His rough thumb and forefinger snuff out the flame. He takes the candle out of my mouth and pours hot wax down the middle of my chest, where it cools and hardens on impact with my shimmery aura.

I scream.

I wipe sweat from my hairline with my forearm, a pair of chopsticks between my fingers. I eat a mouthful of pad Thai as I stare out at the green lake. I think about James, my problematic mentor and my friend, somewhere on this planet. Our bizarre bondage bromance once changed the trajectory of my life. I want some kind of revelation and sense of direction again, so badly, here in Thailand.

As I think about the last bondage scene I played out with James, I wonder how many revelatory moments one person can really be owed.

Maybe people don't need or deserve that many profound, paradigm-shifting experiences. Maybe the lessons life has already handed us need to be put together because the whole is greater than the sum of its parts. Maybe everything I'm still looking for I already have, and maybe everything I need to be I already am. Maybe experience and information are accumulated in linear time but need to flipped over, folded, and looked back at out of sequence to be understood.

A delicate, subjective origami of the soul—all to come to the simple realization that maybe, we're already where we need to be.

It's a passing thought on the banks of a green lake.

I see scales and movement, suddenly, in the water. For a moment, I think it's a crocodile. Living in rural northern Australia has trained me to assume that a croc attack can and will happen. The face of the reptile in the water is smaller than a crocodile's, though. The snout is short. The full length of the reptile is greater than my height. What the hell is in the water? Am I in danger? All my existential musing goes out the window. Where the hell am I? I look around for other people but there's no one around. What do I do?

In the grass a few feet away from me is one of the Silom street kitties. She has wandered into Lumphini Park from across the road. I look from the kitten to the water reptile and back to the kitten again. She's closer to the water's edge than I am, and she seems wholly unconcerned for her own health and safety, so I decide that if she thinks she's okay, then I must be okay. I'm looking to a cat for life-and-death advice. I pull my feet up onto the bench I'm sitting on—as if that will keep me safe—and keep looking to the cat for recommendations until the reptile swims away.

Kyle catches up to me in the park after buying us some bottles of water.

"I just saw I don't know what in the lake. It was about six feet long, and it had scales."

"Oh, it was a monitor lizard! They live in this park!"

"Huge lizards live in this inner-city park?"

"Yes! It's so strange."

"I wasn't sure whether or not I was going to die, and I looked at the cat over there to see whether I should be afraid."

"I wouldn't have suggested this park if it were dangerous."

"Kyle, I may have to re-evaluate what I think I know about life. What do I know, if there are contexts where cats know more than me?"

"It's humbling, isn't it?"

We sit on the bench together and take turns eating pad Thai. Kyle hopes another monitor lizard will come our way. We walk through the park and take touristy photos. We head back to the city streets. We walk past orange-clad Buddhist monks going about their lives, smartphones in hand, taking their own pictures. We visit an art gallery and find a photo essay of the Pope on a visit to Thailand. We cut through alleys and visit another gallery where there's an exhibition of photos of different 7-Elevens from across Thailand at sunset. I try to take nice pictures of Kyle, but they aren't happy with the way they look in any of them. They've been misgendered, misrepresented, and misunderstood so much, so often. Lately, seeing themself in photos just heightens the dysphoria they feel. I wish I could bully the world into being a place that didn't make the person I love most hurt this way. The afternoon heat turns to still-hot dusk on the last day of the decade.

We eat hot ramen noodles at a plastic table just off Sala Daeng, sitting on bright-orange stools along with our LGBTQ cohort. I check Angele Anang's social media again—there's nothing that says she's BKK-bound.

"If we're going to end the decade anywhere tonight, I think we should go to the Stranger Bar. One of the *Drag Race Thailand* contestants from season 2 owns it, and if Pangina Heals or anyone else from the show is going to pop up unexpectedly, it might be there," I say.

We stop in at our hotel, and Kyle does their hair and makeup for our night out. I open a window and lean out to look at the streets of Bangkok, the primary colours of the buildings, the tangled mess of electrical wires that hover above the streets, and the headlights of tuk-tuks passing by, blasting Drake from tinny portable speakers.

We head down one of the alleys of Silom to the Stranger. It's pretty early in the evening, but even so, the drag bar is packed by the time we get there. We hover at the door with an all-cis gay guy crowd who process Kyle as a twink who loves glitter eyeshadow and intermittently process me as either Kyle's fag hag or their lesbian bestie. Even in queer community, in a district of no fucks given, the cisgender gaze tends to box in who people are allowed to be. Kyle and I keep finding the gaps between gays to squeeze our way inside. Fuck what anyone else thinks of us; we see ourselves, we know who we are, and we're going to get to where we need to be.

Inside the bar, the place is slammed. We've been talking and dreaming about coming here for months. In queer worlds, the places we dream of and idolize are always smaller in person. It's a long, narrow black box space with glittery plastic stars stuck to the walls here and there, interspersed with residual Christmas decorations for the benefit of us tourists. Midway through the space, there's a black-railed stairwell leading up to a stage overlooking the dance floor. Under the overhang of the stage, there's a bar where the staff are serving, full throttle, as fast as they can. At the back of the bar there's exactly one all-gender bathroom stall, ensuring that at least half the people here will, at some point throughout the night, be dancing while holding in their pee. I think about the potted plants in the alley outside. "Please, Do Not Pee On Me."

Kyle grabs us some Changs, and we hit the dance floor. We've made it here, we've made it inside, and if nothing else, we're going to dance until the decade ends and a new era begins.

The hours of the night stretch on, and I watch Kyle get looser and looser in their movements. They hardly ever dance, so I love seeing them so free. Drag queens prance up and down the stage stairs. One of the straight guys I used to fuck in BC once asked me why drag matters.

"For us queer people, drag artists are emissaries from the country we need," I answered.

Kyle and I don't talk much. We sink into our own sensory experiences and let the pounding pop tracks pound through us in the crowd of strangers at the Stranger. I give up hope that there will be some big reveal moment of a performer we've been following on TV. I look at Kyle, sweating and dancing, swinging their hair in staccato as they are caught in a strobe-light blitz. They're so fucking beautiful. I breathe easy. They're where they need to be.

Kyle catches me looking at them.

"I'm so glad I met you, and I'm so glad we're here!" they scream over the music.

I check my phone. It's nearly midnight. This is how we're ending the decade.

There's a commotion at the front door of the Stranger. The gays are screaming. I can't see over the heads of the people, but soon, the dance floor parts, out of deference, respect, and love for who has just walked in.

It's some contestants from season 2 of *Drag Race Thailand*, out of drag. They're dragging suitcases behind them across the dance floor, and they look like they've just gotten in from the airport—that dry, sweaty, dishevelled way that everyone looks after they've been on a plane for hours. There's Srimala, followed by Kana Warrior.

Beside me, Kyle suddenly screams.

"Sly! It's Angele Anang! Angele just walked in!"

There's nothing more divine than having a dream, giving up on it, then having it happen. It must be all the luck carried by kittens.

I look at Kyle's face. They're beyond ecstatic. The look on their face says that God is a trans woman, and God just entered the room.

The lid just blows the fuck off the Stranger, as we all realize we're going to ring in the new year with a woman who epitomizes the future of drag and who epitomizes the world we don't live in just yet, but that is coming.

Everyone dances harder, more passionately, and with more abandon. In the stop-start of the strobe lights, we all move, pause, and become photos that will last forever. For a second, the dance floor lights up from below, everyone moves in unison, and every foot on the dance floor lifts into the air simultaneously.

We hear Beyoncé's voice. Angele Anang steps onto the stage. She opens her mouth, and Beyoncé's voice comes out.

As queerdos, kinksters, and trans kids, we are always people within people, living in worlds within worlds. We scrape together enough fishnet, determination, pop culture quotations, and fragments of different philosophies to build lives of practical elegance.

The room sings in unison with Angele, asking what the point is of grinding nine-to-five to stay alive.

Kyle turns to me, in the middle of the song, to scream along.

I grin at them and take their hand so I can kiss the back of it. Seeds of revelation are planting inside them. I can see it.

Angele heads down the stairs of the stage midsong to get closer to her audience. I reach into my pocket, pull out five hundred baht, and stuff it into Kyle's hand.

"Tip Angele!" I scream in their ear.

Kyle holds up the cash as Angele saunters her way down the staircase. She spots the tip and makes her way to Kyle without missing a beat.

Kyle's made of light.

Angele leans over the stair railing, takes the tip from Kyle's fingers, and kisses them on the cheek.

God is a trans woman with the voice of Beyoncé, and Kyle's just been given a sacred blessing. What the blessing is and what it means for Kyle is for them to decide. The club lights hit them, but they beam even brighter. I witness a transcendent moment.

We dance all night, through Angele's extended set, from "Haunted" to "Say My Name."

We dance through Kana Warrior taking the stage and stomping down the staircase like only Kana can.

We dance through Srimala's camp as she spanks the underboob of her own breastplate, over and over. We die with happiness. Her signature underboob titty spanks have been giving us life for months, as we've watched her on TV. It's a gesture full of absurdity, self-love, and resilience, and it's become something we do to ourselves intermittently during our shitty workweeks. It's a silly act that reminds us we're alive and we're not the people our cis co-workers decide to interpret us as. It's an act of silliness that makes us feel like we won't always be so boxed in.

We dance until the dance floor thins out, until the performances are over, until the gay guys that are left are lingering around to see if they can take home any of the performers.

Kyle points out that there's a kitten hugging the walls of the dance floor. The kitty is wearing a tiny blue vest that says "The Stranger" like she's a little, furry employee.

"The cat works here!" Kyle squeals.

Real life is so much stranger than fiction.

I realize Kyle may never leave this bar—but the staff look like they think it would be great if we moved on, so I grab us bottles of water and tell Kyle we should head out. For us, it's been the night of our lives. For the human and feline staff, it's been another night of service. Bartenders at drag bars might be stalwarts of change, but they are also still shift workers. Even nights of transcendence have to end. Outside, dawn is breaking.

We sit on a curb in front of the bar to rehydrate and breathe. The cat employee walks past us.

"I think I'm going to start using she and her pronouns instead of they and them, even though they and them still fit me. That way, if people are going to get it wrong when they address me, at least they're getting it wrong in the right direction. I can't be called he and him anymore," Kyle says, in the early hours of a new decade.

"It's not the first time you've talked to me about using she and her."

"You're right. I forgot about that time hooking up back in Vancouver."

"I think you should do whatever makes sense for you."

"Anything that costs me my sense of who I am ... maybe it's not worth it. There are other lines of work I could do, with my education. There are other careers."

It's the first time I see Kyle address an injustice in her life from a place of resilience and self-love rather than blind panic and fear.

I take another picture of her as she sits outside of the Stranger, while the bar closes down in the background. This time, Kyle likes the way she looks in the photo.

"That looks like the real me."

I tear up for a moment, in the alley in Silom. Maybe the revelatory moments in my story are done for now. I look at Kyle. Maybe hers have just begun.

I wake up in the Shibari Salon next to James, who's sleeping like a big cat beside me. I don't wake him up before I leave. I walk out into the dull morning light on Queen Street. I feel snow settle and melt on my eyelids. The sky baptizes my eyes. I don't understand what that means right now. The seeds of revelation have been buried. They'll begin to bloom by green waters.

READER CONTENT WARNINGS

This memoir is intended for adult readers. It includes:

- intense and frightening scenes
- descriptions of sex, nudity, fetish practices, and sado-masochism
- profanity
- descriptions of smoking and drug, alcohol, and substance misuse
- descriptions of violence and non-consensual sexual violence
- references to self-harm and suicidal ideation
- references to depression and anxiety
- references to coercion and gaslighting
- references to police services and the family court system
- references to child abuse and child sexual abuse
- references to colonialism
- references to unwanted pregnancies
- descriptions of misogyny, homophobia, biphobia, enbyphobia, transphobia, and dysphoria
- reference to violence against animals
- mention of President Donald Trump
- references to FOSTA-SESTA

ACKNOWLEDGMENTS

This work was created with the support of the Canada Council for the Arts and would not have been possible without the professional support of my colleagues:

C.E. Gatchalian, thank you for always pushing me forward.

Matthew DiMera, thank you for having faith in my voice and handing me a megaphone.

Eternity Martis, thank you for walking through the corridors of my mind.

I acknowledge the Wurundjeri and Boon Wurrung peoples of the Kulin Nation as the owners of the unceded land on which this book was written.

SLY is a writer and performance artist from Tiohtià:ke/Montreal, now based in Naarm/Melbourne. They work as cabin crew for a budget airline and pursue contentment through incessant meal planning, doing Yoga with Adriene, making love like a beast, and making out in Melbourne's many laneways. Sly moved to Tkaronto/ Toronto when they were fourteen, went to high school with Drake, and through the 2000s and 2010s worked in IT and in call centres. Amid three-hour weekday commutes on the TTC and weekends of finger-banging in bathrooms on Church Street, they got into making art through queer platforms like Videofag, Buddies in Bad Times Theatre, and *Xtra Magazine*. These days, when Sly isn't in the sky, they run a performance collective called Tender Container, which is developing Canada's first all-trans and non-binary performance anthology for Playwrights Canada Press.

tendercontainer.com